DATE DUE

Complete
Hydrangeas

Complete
Hydrangeas

Glyn Church

FIREFLY BOOKS

Acknowledgments

My thanks to Graham Smith for opening my eyes to
hydrangeas; to Gail Church for her patience and help
with flower colors; Tracey Borgfeldt, Joy Browne, Astral
Sligo and Paul Bateman for editing and producing this
book. For their fantastic photos, a very special thank you
to Pat Greenfield, Gil Hanly, Tim Wood, Ryoji Irie, Luc
Balemans, Mal Condon, Judith King, Tom Mills, Koos and
Wilko Hofstede. For plants, information and photos my
thanks also to Robert and Corinne Mallet, Mal and Mary
Kay Condon, Satoki Matsui, Takeomi Yamamoto, Donald
McPherson, Maurice Foster, Robert Bett, Reinier van
Rijssen, Michael and Carola Hudson, Tom Hudson, Brian
and Chris Evans, Roy Treherne, Sheila Robertson, Sarah
Davey, Lady Anne Berry, Bruce and Margaret Willan,
Ozzie Johnson, David Newman, Helen Carryer, Michael
Dirr, the late Os Blumhardt and Penny McHenry.
And my thanks, as always, to Joni Mitchell for the music
to write to.

FRONT COVER: Hydrangea macrophylla 'Enziandom'
BACK COVER: Hydrangea macrophylla 'Masja'
PAGE 1: Hydrangea macrophylla 'Romance'
PAGE 2: Hydrangea macrophylla 'Nikko Blue'
PAGE 3: Hydrangea paniculata 'Grandiflora'
PAGE 4: Hydrangea macrophylla 'Penny Mac' in the
front garden of the late Penny McHenry, founder of the
American Hydrangea Society.
OPPOSITE (from top): Hydrangea macrophylla 'Beauté
Vendômise'; *H. arborescens* 'Annabelle'; *H. macrophylla*
'Eternity'; *H. scandens*; *H. macrophylla* 'Henrich Seidal'
PAGES 6–7: Hydrangea macrophylla 'Montgomery'

A FIREFLY BOOK

Published by Firefly Books Ltd. 2007

First printing

Publisher Cataloging-in-Publication Data (U.S.)

Church, Glyn.
   Complete hydrangeas / Glyn Church.
[144] p. : col. photos. ; cm.
Includes bibliographical references and index.
Summary: Hydrangea species and cultivars, with their
history in cultivation, their growing requirements and
their landscaping potential.
ISBN-13: 978-1-55407-263-7 (pbk.)
ISBN-10: 1-55407-263-8 (pbk.)
1. Hydrangeas. 2. Hydrangeas—Varieties.
3. Landscape gardening. I. Title.
635.9/3372 dc22   SB413.H93.C48   2007

Library and Archives Canada Cataloguing in Publication

Church, Glyn
   Complete hydrangeas / Glyn Church. – 1st ed.
Includes bibliographical references and index.
ISBN-13: 978-1-55407-263-7
ISBN-10: 1-55407-263-8
   1. Hydrangeas. I. Title.
SB413.H93C48   2007635.9'3372   C2006-906863-1

Published in the United States by
Firefly Books (U.S.) Inc.
P.O. Box 1338, Ellicott Station
Buffalo, New York 14205

Published in Canada by
Firefly Books Ltd.
66 Leek Crescent
Richmond Hill, Ontario L4B 1H1

First published in 2007 by
David Bateman Ltd,
30 Tarndale Grove,
Albany, Auckland, New Zealand

Designed by Intesa Group, Auckland, New Zealand
Printed in China through Colorcraft Ltd., Hong Kong

CONTENTS

Introduction

Hydrangeas work well in
formal planting.

Hydrangeas are back in fashion after a few decades of being ignored. I find it
hard to fathom why their popularity ever waned when they have so many wonderful qualities. Hydrangeas can be everything from formal shrubs in a court-
yard to the visual highlight of a woodland garden. If you only have a paved
area, or perhaps no garden at all, you can still enjoy hydrangeas in containers,
maybe as window box subjects in an apartment, as a flowering potted plant
on your dining table, or in vases around your living areas. No other plant is so
diverse, so resilient or gives such pleasure for so long.

Over the years hydrangeas have won me over completely. From initially
thinking of these plants as simply a fill-in shrub for summer color, I now see
hidden depths and qualities in every one. This has driven me to some lengths to
acquire new hydrangeas; everything from importing new varieties to extend the
range available, to trekking through remote regions and abandoned homesteads

looking for old faithfuls that have survived the centuries. The old house may fall down and disintegrate, but next to its foundations the ever-resilient hydrangea lives on. In this quest I've been extremely fortunate to have had the help of Corinne and Robert Mallet in France, Mal and Mary Kay Condon in the United States and Maurice Foster in England. All these enthusiasts have introduced me to new plants and sent me material. In New Zealand I was indebted to the late Os Blumhardt, who kept an old labeled collection of hydrangeas long after most people would have dug them out as "unfashionable." With Os's help I've been able to restore some long-lost varieties to Europe and the United States. I've also trekked around the world searching for wild hydrangeas in Korea, China, and the Himalayas. In Bhutan we found hydrangea plants as big as old pear trees. Not only were they large enough to climb, but on one occasion I observed langur monkeys among their branches, teasing a yapping dog below.

Someone in the United States (Martha Stewart, I think) decided in the year 1999 to call the hydrangea "the plant of the next millennium." I would be delighted to think these shrubs could be popular for the next thousand years, and with the never-ending range of colors and new cultivars available, there's no reason that this can't be prophetic.

The macrophylla type of hydrangea has a new-found popularity, primarily for two reasons. Firstly, the shrubs are now appreciated as exceptional providers of long-lasting cut flowers to decorate homes throughout the year. Secondly, for garden use, growers have discovered what are called "remontant" varieties capable of sending up new flower stalks all summer. In cold regions flowering canes may die in winter, or the early flowers are frosted and killed in spring, resulting in no flowers during the months following. Now, with the remontant types sending up new flower stems from below the frosted buds, even people in cold regions can enjoy hydrangeas in their garden. People like Michael Dirr, professor of horticulture at the University of Georgia in Atlanta, have set up extensive breeding programs to find hardier cultivars and ones resistant to common diseases. There has also been a huge increase in the number and popularity of *H. paniculata* and *H. quercifolia* as these are more reliably hardy and will therefore grow in more regions of the country. This has encouraged nurserymen to look for new clones of these species and has given us some splendid new varieties to grace our gardens—doubles, pinks and bicolored forms, all adding to the hydrangea's appeal.

In Japan, the home of many hydrangeas, the shrubs were long seen as inconstant because they can change color depending on the soil type in which they grow. Despite this limitation, their popularity continues with the Japanese, who are now introducing a host of delicious double-flowered lacecaps in both the macrophylla and serrata series. It seems that all over the world these classic garden shrubs are enjoying a renaissance.

FROM TOP: *Hydrangea paniculata* 'Kyushu'; *H. quercifolia* 'Snow Queen'; *H. macrophylla* showing the classic mophead shape and the range of colors that can sometimes be seen on individual plants.

Where Do Hydrangeas Come From?

Over the past three centuries, hydrangeas, like most other garden plants, have been modified and hybridized to create new colorful treats for gardeners.

The popular mophead varieties we grow for cut flowers and garden decoration first came to Europe from Japan and China. Back in 1879 a man by the name of Charles Maries was sent to China and Japan by the famous Veitch Nursery near Exeter, on the south coast of England. History hasn't been too kind to Maries; he's often described as lazy and unenterprising, but perhaps he just didn't have the same dogged determination of some who came after him. Yet traveling in strange countries where every foreigner was regarded with suspicion at the very least, and often with loathing and hatred, Maries to my mind did pretty well to come away with the bones of a hydrangea industry that now grows literally millions of plants per year. However, at the time neither he nor his hydrangeas were appreciated.

Maries brought back two hydrangeas from Japan. One was a lacecap type, a form of the coastal *Hydrangea macrophylla*. It was appropriately called *H. m.* 'Mariesii' and is still available today, so it has stood the test of time. The other was a round, dome-headed form of *H. serrata* and was named *H. s.* 'Rosea'.

OPPOSITE: *Hydrangea macrophylla* has a lacecap flower—the true flowers are the dark blue center, surrounded by light blue to white sterile flowers. In front is 'Princess Beatrix', a classic mophead *macrophylla* cultivar.
RIGHT: Self-seeded *Hydrangea macrophylla* plants.

ABOVE: *Hydrangea macrophylla* 'Générale Vicomtesse de Vibraye.'

RIGHT: *Hydrangea serrata* 'Miyama-yae-Murasaki' (syn. 'Purple Tiers') being a serrata variety is hardier than the macrophylla types, but does prefer some shade.

For reasons that are hard to fathom, the Veitch people were not enamored of these hydrangeas, but luckily for us they did eventually offer them to colleagues in France.

A Monsieur A. Truffaut took them to France, where they were exhibited by the Société Nationale d'Horticulture in Paris in 1901. From that point on the French were hooked and their horticulturists have bred hydrangeas with great dedication ever since.

The French Lemoine Brothers discovered mophead hydrangeas have a few true flowers within and they set about breeding them. Before long two other French nurserymen, Messieurs Mouillère and Cayeux, had joined the race to breed new exotic hydrangeas for indoor decoration. This explains why so many of our popular hydrangeas have such long French names, e.g. 'Générale Vicomtesse de Vibraye' and 'Souvenir du Président Paul Doumer'. (Nowadays a cultivar is allowed only three names for the sake of simplicity and brevity, and so the latter is usually sold as 'Président Doumer'.)

Subsequently Belgian, Dutch, German and Swiss breeders have joined the quest for the ideal hydrangea, and for most of these breeders perfection is a superb potted plant or indoor plant. Many hydrangeas were bred for forcing as early summer-flowering potted plants for sale throughout Europe. This trade continues unabated throughout the world, where growers using artificial light and chilling techniques can now persuade the plants to flower at any time of the year.

The very first hydrangea to be discovered and introduced to Western gardens was the North American *H. arborescens* and this too didn't generate much excitement in the plant world. Collected by John Bartram in the 1730s, and

later described in *Flora Virginica*, 1739, it charmed a few English plant fanatics and was then forgotten for generations.

John Bartram (1699–1777) was the son of a cantankerous Quaker farmer who was excommunicated by his church and later tragically killed by Indians. John and his brother were then raised by their grandparents. Despite the tough pioneer life, John prospered as a farmer and raised a large family. In many ways he was a typical colonial, with day-to-day farming skills but no education or ambition beyond raising a family. One day he bought a book about plants and it changed his life; he became the most prominent botanist in all the New World.

Despite being terrified of Indians after his father's demise, he began trekking through the wilds of the Appalachian Mountains. Alone and mostly on foot, he scoured these hills long before the explorations of Daniel Boone and other famous woodsmen. His journeys took him as far south as Florida. He was fortunate in several ways; he never came to any serious harm and his search was not in vain as he found a correspondent in England who wanted plants from the new colony.

Peter Collinson, a rich London merchant, was desperate to find a botanist in

Hydrangea macrophylla 'Tokyo Delight' is one of the few hydrangeas to have colored leaves in the fall, which could indicate some serrata influence in its parentage.

Hydrangea paniculata 'Praecox', a wild form of the species.

the colonies who would be willing to send him plants and seeds. Bartram was commissioned to send a box of plants and seeds to Collinson for five guineas, and the American plant hunter subsequently sent hundreds of boxes during the next 30 years to the ever-enthusiastic Londoner. Collinson sent him books on botany as well as the regular stipend. Books were very scarce in the colonies and much appreciated by Bartram.

To share the cost, Collinson sold shares in Bartram's "boxes" to wealthy patrons, the landed gentry of England, and later, thanks to Collinson's influence, Bartram was to attain the honor of being appointed as "botanist" to King George III.

Both men became famous in their own country; Europeans credit Collinson with importing vast numbers of plants, while Americans regard Bartram as the "first" American botanist.

In later years John Bartram's son, William, accompanied him on his travels. Among many other botanical treasures, they discovered *H. quercifolia*. This cream-flowered species is native to Georgia. Father and son set up a five-acre botanic garden at Bartram's home on the Schuylkill River and today this garden is part of the Philadelphia Parks Department.

Meanwhile, across the world in Japan, hydrangeas were discovered and categorized as elderberries and later as viburnums by European botanists. In their defense, these botanists were extremely limited in what they could achieve as

Japan had basically banned all foreigners in an attempt to keep out European culture and religions.

The Dutch East India Company was allowed a very small base on Deshima Island and from here they were permitted to carry out some limited trading. Traveling to the other side of the known world in tiny ships was a risky business and the company sent doctors on the ships and based some of them in Japan. Doctors are inherently interested in botany, for many cures come from botanical sources. A physician working for the company, Engelbert Kaempfer (1651–1715), was the first man to discover and describe the Asian hydrangeas, though he is rarely credited with this. He included them in the *Sambucus* or elderberry group of plants.

The staff of the Dutch East India Company was not allowed on the mainland and Kaempfer found this restriction incredibly frustrating. However, once a year a delegation from the company had to pay homage to the Emperor's court in Tokyo, then known as Edo, and this gave him a golden opportunity to botanize. It was during one of these trips that he found hydrangeas.

Nearly 100 years later, Carl Peter Thunberg (1743–1828), a Swedish physician, held the same post with the Dutch East India Company and had to comply with the same travel restrictions. Frustrated at not being allowed off the island to search for new species, he devised a cunning plan to acquire mainland plants. Thunberg kept a goat, and on the pretext of collecting fodder for this animal, his Japanese servants were allowed to go and harvest greenery and hay on the mainland. Among this "goat fodder" were two plants Thunberg described as *Viburnum macrophyllum*, a tough coastal plant, and *V. serratum*, a smaller woodland plant variety. It turned out that these two plants were in fact hydrangeas, so when they were later transferred to the hydrangea genus, they kept the species names Thunberg had used, thus giving us *H. macrophylla* and *H. serrata*.

The next plant-hunter physician working for the Dutch and also based on Deshima Island was Philipp Franz von Siebold (1797–1866). A German by birth, he was an eye specialist as well as a physician.

His oculist skills allowed him onto the Japanese mainland to visit patients, on which occasions he casually "botanized" along the way. Based in Japan for six years, from 1823 to 1829, he wrote *Flora Japonica* about the plants he discovered, including several new species of hydrangea.

Whereas Siebold's predecessors were interested only in Japanese plants, Siebold became besotted by everything Japanese. In effect, he became Japanese; he married a Japanese woman and immersed himself in the culture. He also studied Japanese art and geography.

His passion overwhelmed him and he went too far, persuading a Japanese astronomer friend to part with a map of Japan and the mainland province

BELOW: The very different looks of *Hydrangea macrophylla* 'Princess Juliana' (top) and a wild form of *H. serrata* with hostas in the foreground.

ABOVE: A classic mophead, *Hydrangea macrophylla* 'Heinrich Seidel'.

ABOVE RIGHT: The lacecap flower of *Hydrangea macrophylla* 'Zaunkönig'.

of Amur. To the Japanese authorities maps were secret documents, as maps equaled knowledge for possible invaders.

During a short coastal trip, Siebold's ship ran aground and the map was discovered. Some collaborators were put to death and Siebold for his part was imprisoned and eventually banished from Japan forever. It must have been a cruel blow for someone so entranced by the country. He was not to return to the country for 30 years.

Finally, in 1859, Siebold was granted his heart's desire, the chance to return to Japan. Imagine his joy—not only was he allowed to return to his beloved Japan, but he became an adviser to the Japanese government. The government saw him as a key to understanding foreigners. Naturally, this upset the Dutch East India Company, who now perceived him to be a spy. But to Siebold this was heaven; he could live on the mainland, spend his days botanizing and embrace his adopted culture. However his joy was short-lived. Three years later the company tricked him into traveling to Java on a diplomatic mission. Once Siebold was out of the country, the Dutch would not allow him to go back to Japan, and so he returned to Europe, heartbroken.

All of our ornamental hydrangeas come from Japan, China or the eastern United States (in the Appalachian mountain chain). There are many genera, families of plants, common to these three regions as millions of years ago they were linked in a single land mass. There are hydrangea species, and the related Dichroas, growing in Vietnam, Bhutan and Nepal, and also Mexico and South America, but few have made it into cultivation.

Hydrangea flowers

Most flowers have showy petals to attract insects to pollinate the flower and perpetuate the species. Hydrangeas are deceivers, for what we think of as their petals are not petals at all but sepals. Let me explain. A typical flower, such as a rose, opens from a bud. This bud is protected from the elements by tough green bracts or sepals. When the flower is ready to open, these sepals peel back and the delicate petals emerge. Once the flower is open, insects come, and pollination takes place. When the ovary accepts the pollen the flower has done its job and the petals fade away. In a wild hydrangea the true flowers capable of producing seeds are very small and insignificant. The plant has come up with a trick to attract insects by providing "pretend" flowers. These showy pretend flowers are made up of sepals, those tough scales that are green on a rose flower, but in the case of a hydrangea can be red, white or blue.

Let's look at the flowers of *H. macrophylla*, the shrub we think of as a typical hydrangea. The flowers come in two shapes, *lacecaps* and *mopheads*. Lacecaps are the wild plant version. They're called lacecaps because of the similarity to the lacy cap worn by Victorian housemaids in the stately homes of England. The flower is flat, with an outer circle of pretend flowers made from sepals; inside is a mass of tiny true flowers. Insects are attracted by the larger pretend flowers and, having been enticed, will then pollinate the true flowers in the center. Much to nearly everyone's surprise, a lot of hydrangea flowers are scented and this helps attract insects too. Like all flowers, they fade when pollinated and so lacecap flowers are fairly short lived. The outer pretend flowers have one last trick before they fade; each sepal turns 180 degrees and changes color, say from white to red or red to green.

In the case of a typical mophead hydrangea, there are no petals and also no true flowers—or at least very few. They are made up almost entirely of pretend sepal flowers. Because there are no real flowers to pollinate, the sepal flowers live on and on. This explains why the flowers of mophead hydrangeas last for up to six months while most flowers have a short lifespan of one or two weeks. It's easy to see how this shrub's flowers came by the name of "mophead," for they look so much like an old-fashioned kitchen mop used for cleaning floors.

Most wild hydrangeas have flat lacecap flowers. Some species like *H. paniculata* and *H. quercifolia* have pointy panicle-like flowers, but they are still made up of small true flowers with a few larger pretend flowers to attract pollinating insects.

The true flowers account for how hydrangeas were named. People often imagine these shrubs got their name from an association with water, as some of these plants prefer wet conditions. This assumption is only partly correct. The name was bestowed because the true flowers are shaped like a Greek urn or water vessel. In Greek, "hydra" means water and "angeion" is a vessel. Many of our so-called Latin names are derived from Greek.

Hydrangea paniculata
'Grandiflora'

The genus is *Hydrangea*, the species name is *macrophylla*, and the variety or cultivar name is 'Madame Plumecoq'.

Plant names

Gardeners often complain about complicated Latin names and ask why do we need them, and why not use common names instead. Fortunately for gardeners with an aversion to Latin, some plants' names have become so commonplace that we don't even realize they are in Latin. Hydrangea is one such name, being both the Latin and common name for this group of plants. Dahlia, chrysanthemum, fuchsia, lobelia and even rosa are all Latin names we take for granted and use as common names too.

In the United States and Canada common names for plants seem to be remarkably consistent from region to region, whereas in England and Europe a plant will go by a different name every ten miles down the road. So we use Latin names for consistency, and it's especially useful when talking to people from other countries. It's fascinating to be among a group of horticulturists from all over the world and realize the discussion is taking place using unifying Latin names.

If you think Latin is complicated now, then just imagine how it was before the arrival of Carl Linnaeus, the inventor of the current system. Prior to Linnaeus, plant names were more like a sentence in Latin. By comparison, the Linnaeus binomial or two-name system is much simpler and it works for all living things such as birds, insects, plants and animals. The first or *genus* name is like our surname, bringing a related group together, while the *species* name is a bit like our given name. So in the case of hydrangeas growing as far away as China, Japan and eastern North America, the Latin name unites them because they are so closely related. Then the species name separates them and should, theoretically, describe them, so *H. paniculata* has panicles; *H. quercifolia* has oak-like leaves, indicated by the use of *quercus*, the Latin for oak; and so on.

Botanists discern what grouping a plant belongs to by its flowers. The logic is that as they are short-lived, flowers don't need to modify themselves to the environmental conditions such as cold or drought, therefore the flowers should look very similar to other close relatives.

Sometimes botanists will give a third Latin name to a plant to distinguish it from other very close relatives and this is called a *subspecies*. In the hydrangea genus we have a lot of different forms of *H. aspera* such as *H. a.* subsp. *villosa*, which with its hairy leaves and lilac lacecap flowers is well known. One of its very close allies is *H. a.* subsp. *sargentiana*, which has enormous hairy leaves and huge lacecap flowers. For gardeners it's easy to see the difference between these two close relatives, but for a botanist the flowers are very very similar and so they are separated only by the subspecies names. To save time and space we abbreviate the name "hydrangea" to a capital H. and the species name "aspera" to a lower case a. In this way the important bit—*villosa*—is also emphasized.

In addition, we have *cultivars* or *varieties*; these are good garden forms of wild plants. Someone has spotted a seedling that is much better than its siblings and given it a *variety* or *cultivar* name. A good example is *H. paniculata* 'Grandiflora' or the peegee hydrangea. The cultivars must be propagated by cuttings or grafting to ensure each plant is identical to the original plant. (If you were to sow seed from a cultivar you would have a mixture of offspring, just as you would if you sowed the pips from an apple.)

Hybrids are plants grown from seed originally. Usually someone cross-pollinates two plants and saves the seed, but the pollination can be natural, by bees and other insects. From the resulting seedlings, the best clones are selected and if good enough will be named.

Hydrangea quercifolia showing its oak-like leaves, hence the species name from 'quercus', Latin for oak.

The Charm of Hydrangeas

Hydrangeas have so many winning attributes, it's hard to imagine an easier group of plants to grow, or any other flowering shrubs capable of providing vibrant color for so long a season. With the possible exception of roses, hydrangeas flower for longer than any other group of woody plants. As a bonus, these shrubs give us superb cut flowers in high summer and wonderful dried blooms for winter. Many hydrangeas have fragrant flowers, giving a heady, honey-like scent to be enjoyed on your garden rambles. Some hydrangeas can climb, making them useful for covering unsightly walls, fences and even old tree stumps or water tanks. Added to all this, hydrangeas don't grow too big and will fit in virtually any garden. If by chance a hydrangea seems too large for the site you've chosen, you can move the plant the following fall or winter, or perhaps try modifying the height with a pruning regime.

You may think your garden is too small for hydrangeas, but space is not hard to find. There are many dwarf varieties suited to confined situations. Homeowners with just a small deck or concrete patio can grow a few of these in containers. Planted in attractive pots or tubs, they make a grand job of softening the hard edges of timber and concrete. Hydrangeas are so adaptable you can even grow them if you live in an apartment. The majority of hydrangea plants sold around the world are grown as potted plants. For indoor decoration they

OPPOSITE: A mass display of *Hydrangea quercifolia* in Nancy McCabe's garden in Connecticut, USA.

RIGHT: *Hydrangea macrophylla* 'Masja' has red mopheads that fade to a metallic antique color.

are superb subjects. A beautiful mop-top hydrangea will grace your table or mantle for months. Another possibility is to grow them in window boxes. One of my jobs as a young horticulturist was to decorate the homes of the rich and famous in London. At five in the morning we would go to the old Dickensian Covent Garden market to buy hydrangeas and geraniums to plant in window boxes and create mini gardens, "Swiss style," outside every window of an apartment. Hydrangeas tolerate wind and poor weather, making them ideal for this tough situation, and of course their long flowering season makes them perfectly suited for such a role.

Being easy-to-grow shrubs has to be a major benefit of planting hydrangeas, for gardeners always like to be successful. So many plants come with a proviso—"Oh, it's a really good plant except it gets black spot..." for example. Grow hydrangeas and you can relax. There's no need to worry about spraying for bugs every week or so, and no long-term problems with dieback or disease. Talk about easy care; hydrangeas can be left alone from the day you plant them and still they will succeed. Of course, your plants will certainly perform better if you feed, prune and mulch them, but it isn't essential.

Let's look at some hydrangeas' attributes in detail.

Long-lasting color

Hydrangeas, especially the macrophylla types, are simply brilliant for providing garden color over a very long season. When all the spring-flowering shrubs have gone into growth mode the hydrangeas begin to flower and go on and on all summer, giving us a stunning show. We have a great range of colors to choose from: especially good creams and whites; pinks from pastel to shocking; vibrant shades of red and purple; soft powder blues and rich sea blues. What's more, these flowerheads are not shy; you never have to go searching for the blossoms on a hydrangea. Instead they smother the bush, sometimes completely hiding the leaves, and many appear to be hollering "Look at me!" Some species of hydrangeas are a bit more subtle but still provide a great display.

Most of us know hydrangeas can change their flower color according to the soil, but not many gardeners realize they can also change color from one year to another, or even from one season to another. The mopheads, and to a lesser extent the lacecaps, still provide color well into winter. When the cool nights of fall arrive, the flowers have this remarkable ability to change color. As the blooms age, their large sepals turn turtle and transform themselves into new, exciting colors. Cut-flower growers call this the "antique" phase because the blooms now have an aged, almost timeless look about them. Some of the changes are quite dramatic. Whites can become a fiery red but more often subside into a subtle soft green; bright blues can turn to wine red, purples change to metallic hues and reds usually deepen or darken.

Hydrangeas provide color all summer. Planted next to a house, they may get additional lime from concrete foundations, which helps to keep them red.

ABOVE: White
hydrangeas are a
good choice for shady
locations, as they are less
likely to be damaged by
strong sun or rain.

ABOVE RIGHT:
Hydrangeas are an ideal
shrub with plenty of
colors for mixed borders.

Some purists regard the color changes manifested by hydrangeas to be an impediment to good garden design. If you want to live in a world where everything is constant and repetitive, don't grow hydrangeas. For me, I'm grateful for any shrub capable of flowering all summer for virtually no effort on my part, and if it wants to be white in the summer and green in the fall, then I'll embrace that change.

Foliage fireworks

While most hydrangeas do not have fall-colored leaves, there are two exceptions. Leaves of the serrata hydrangeas take on red, orange and even purple hues in the fall. However, the most exciting are those of *H. quercifolia*, capable of transforming themselves from an average dull green to scintillating burgundy, bronze and burnished reds. Even though their flowers may have been rewarding for months, you'll still be riveted by *H. quercifolia's* leaf colors in fall, when as a bonus the white flowers also take on delicious soft pink tinges. *H. paniculata* blossoms also take on these pink tints in fall and will be good cut flowers at this stage.

Versatile garden subjects

Hydrangeas are amazingly versatile shrubs. If you don't have the time or energy to grow annuals and herbaceous perennials, then hydrangeas will be the mainstay of your summer garden. It's possible to grow them in combination with perennials. Most of the hydrangea species with their lacy or panicle-type flowers look good in a woodland garden, but are equally at home at the back of a mixed or herbaceous border.

The macrophylla types are even more versatile. The lacecaps look good in mixed borders, as a background to roses or perennials, or perhaps in groups of threes, fives or more under trees. The mopheads have an uncanny knack of fitting into formal and informal gardens.

Mopheads can be dotted about in mixed borders or along driveways and so enhance an informal design, but they look equally good in formal settings where their rounded heads and matching rounded bush shape make them the perfect plant. Featured either side of an entranceway, regularly spaced along paths or marching beneath walls, their symmetry is ideal. In times past the French and Italians made exquisite formal gardens to show man had conquered nature and one of the plants they employed was the hydrangea. Years later the English style of natural-looking gardens came into vogue and again hydrangeas were a valued addition to the scene.

Easy-care plants

There is another important aspect to the versatility of hydrangeas; they will grow just about anywhere. Having the ability to cope with sun, shade, wind and weather is a great asset for any plant. Most of the hydrangea species are happy in full sun as long as your climate is not too hot or dry. In full sun the macrophylla types will need a mulch or regular irrigation as they are such thirsty plants, but then they compensate by being such good shade plants. Very few shrubs thrive in shade; H. macrophylla not only copes, but still manages to flower. These shrubs

Few flowering shrubs thrive in shade, but *Hydrangea macrophylla* will flower happily in these conditions.

even survive in very tough windy places too, including salt-laden coastal gardens. The other species do prefer a sheltered site.

Hydrangeas are not overly fussy about soil conditions and will grow in less than perfect earth. Unusually for any group of shrubs, they cope with both acid and alkaline soils. (Nearly all shrubs need an acid or neutral soil and very few survive or relish high alkalinity.) And once planted, hydrangeas demand very little attention. Even if you never touched them again, they would most likely thrive and put on a fantastic show every summer. If you want them to give of their best, then a good deep mulch of bark and an occasional feed would help. They will perform better and exceed your expectations if you give them favorable and kindly treatment. You can prune the macrophylla and paniculata types every winter, but they'll forgive you if you forget, and will still flower for you the next summer. And what's more, the pruning is easy—nothing complex here, and no thorns!

As they suffer from virtually no pests or diseases, hydrangeas are an ideal choice for busy people who don't have the time to be fussing over their plants. If you find yourself in this situation, there's another aspect of the *H. macrophylla* types that will appeal to you. These shrubs are good weed suppressors, their dense foliage keeping out the light needed for unwanted plants to germinate. If you have mulched initially to reduce weeds, the shrubs will smother the soil as they grow, and no weeds will stand a chance thereafter.

Cultivation

To simplify this advice I am treating *Hydrangea macrophylla* and *H. serrata* as one group. I shall then consider the other species, such as *H. paniculata* and *H. quercifolia*, as another group, for they have very different requirements.

Hydrangea macrophylla and *H. serrata*

First, let's look at all the places in which you can successfully grow the above species. They are more tender than other hydrangeas because they live naturally in coastal regions (*H. macrophylla*) and slightly colder mountainous regions of Japan and Korea (*H. serrata*). It's important to know if they will thrive in your area before we consider factors such as soil type, drainage and irrigation—all of which we can influence or change. Although more vulnerable to cold, these species compensate by growing in situations other shrubs can't abide.

Ideally, these hydrangeas would prefer semi-shade or a situation where they get dappled light or sun for say half a day. Surprisingly, they will cope with all-day shade and even fairly dense deciduous shade. As long as the shade is not too dense they will even grow at the base of an old tree trunk. The only drawback is the more shade you give, the more spindly the plants will be and you will have far fewer flowers and probably poorer quality blooms.

In many regions these hydrangeas will grow in full sun if given the right soil

OPPOSITE: *Hydrangea macrophylla* growing well in dappled sunlight. White-flowered varieties especially look their best in these conditions.

RIGHT: *Hydrangea serrata* 'Blue Deckle'

Hydrangeas make good container plants for a patio.

conditions. The key is to have enough moisture to sustain the big fleshy leaves and flowers, especially those of the big mophead types that absorb a huge amount of water. They do enjoy a wet climate, preferably more than 40 in. (100 cm) of rain and ideally above 60 in. (150 cm). If your rainfall is intermittent, you can improve your chances of success by installing an irrigation system to water them during the dry spells. While these tough plants will grow almost anywhere, you will have more success and better blooms if you keep the plants moist.

Most shrubs won't grow in wet or boggy soils, and gardeners often have a struggle to find suitable plants for pond and stream edges. The macrophylla types can handle these wet soils. That's not to say it's ideal for them, but usually they will cope. If I were planting in this situation, I would make an effort to improve the drainage or even aid the flow of the water so it's not stagnant. This adaptability does allow us to plant stream sides and pond edges with something other than perennials. The serrata types do not thrive in wet soils.

Found naturally in coastal regions in their native Japan, the macrophylla types even grow right by the sea. Their tough, glossy leaves allow them to succeed in coastal sites where most shrubs would be destroyed by wind and salt. This is part of the reason they became popular as shrubs for seaside gardens.

Another situation some gardeners struggle with is windy sites; this may just be a windy corner where buildings create a wind tunnel or it may be more drastic, such as a cliff top exposed to salt-laden winds. Surprisingly, *H. macrophylla* types will cope with this too. Certainly some cultivars are more resistant than others; the ones with the shiny glossy leaves are the most resilient. *H. macrophylla* species are without doubt some of the best shrubs for coastal gardens, shrugging off the constant winds and gales. Installing an irrigation system will help them cope with the loss of moisture due to the drying winds.

Let's face it—gardeners struggling with shady corners, wet soil or windy sites would settle for almost any plant capable of growing in these difficult situations. Flowers would be a bonus, but only a secondary consideration. In *H. macrophylla* not only do we have a flowering plant happy to fill these difficult spots but, even more satisfyingly, it's a shrub capable of producing flowers for nearly half the year.

From the foregoing you can see it's possible to grow a hydrangea virtually anywhere as long as your winter temperatures are not too cold. Now we must discuss the biggest drawback to growing these hydrangeas. *H. macrophylla* comes from the coastal regions of Japan and will tolerate cold winters down to only USDA Zone 6 or even 7. There are cold places where the plants will just survive, but this is very different from having a thriving shrub covered in blossom. Therefore, for many gardeners around the world, growing this species successfully is only a dream. Even if the cold doesn't kill the roots it can kill their bud-bearing canes and so prevent any subsequent flowering for the upcoming summer. (Most *H. macrophylla* plants bloom on old wood grown the previous summer and if these are killed then no flowers will appear in subsequent months.)

Happily, over recent years someone noticed that a few *H. macrophylla* varieties were capable of producing new flowering stems throughout the growing season. Such varieties are called *remontant*, which literally means "blooming more than once in the same season." Some old varieties like 'Générale Vicomtesse de Vibraye' and 'Nikko Blue' are capable of doing this. There are also some new cultivars especially selected to repeat flower in this way and so expand the areas in which macrophylla types can be grown. 'Penny Mac', named after the lovely Penny McHenry, founder of the American Hydrangea Society, is one. Another is 'Endless Summer', now causing a real stir in American gardening circles.

There are one or two techniques we can employ to improve our chances of having *H. macrophylla* flower in colder climates. The first and possibly best method of reducing winter damage is to grow the shrubs under the shade of big trees. An overhead canopy is often enough to ward off heavy frosts. Another possibility is to grow them under the eaves of the house where the warm wall and slight overhead protection will increase the immediate temperature. If you have the benefit of owning a very large garden, you may be able to site your hydrangeas near the top of a slope where the frost doesn't settle. (Cold air naturally flows downhill and so it's much colder at the bottom of the slope than it is at the top.)

TOP: 'Nikko Blue' is a remontant macrophylla variety, meaning that it will bloom more than once in a season.

ABOVE: 'Penny Mac' is a new cultivar especially selected to repeat flower throughout the season.

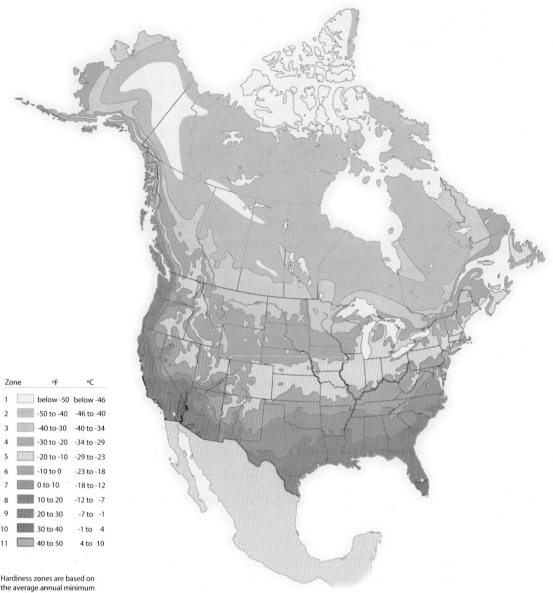

Zone		°F	°C
1		below -50	below -46
2		-50 to -40	-46 to -40
3		-40 to -30	-40 to -34
4		-30 to -20	-34 to -29
5		-20 to -10	-29 to -23
6		-10 to 0	-23 to -18
7		0 to 10	-18 to -12
8		10 to 20	-12 to -7
9		20 to 30	-7 to -1
10		30 to 40	-1 to 4
11		40 to 50	4 to 10

Hardiness zones are based on the average annual minimum temperature for each zone.

This hardiness zone map has been prepared to agree with a system of plant hardiness zones that have been accepted as an international standard and range from 1 to 11. It shows the minimum winter temperatures that can be expected on average in different regions.

Even by changing your pruning times you can reduce the risk of cold damage. Delay pruning the hydrangeas until very late in the spring when the risk of frost is reduced. The canopy of old dead flowerheads from last summer acts as a blanket over the plant, keeping some frost at bay. Spring frosts are more damaging than winter ones because the plants will have already started to grow. If you have only a few hydrangea shrubs you could make an effort to cover them with old blankets or burlap on cold nights to ward off the frost. Some people go to great lengths, constructing cages filled with leaves or straw to protect the plants. As a last resort, you can grow them in large containers and move them indoors over winter. As the plants are deciduous in winter they won't need much light or water, but don't let them dry out completely.

H. serrata types are a little more winter hardy than most macrophylla, being indigenous to colder mountainous areas, and if you live in a cold region it may pay to "practice" with these types before you start planting the more tender *H. macrophylla*. Some *H. serrata* cultivars are remontant too, such as 'Glyn Church'. In a mild climate this variety will keep producing new flowers up until mid-winter.

Other hydrangea species

Most of the other hydrangea types are much more winter hardy and tolerate more cold than the *H. macrophylla* and *H. serrata*. *H. arborescens* will grow to Zone 3, *H. paniculata* Zone 3, *H. quercifolia* Zone 5 and some *H. aspera* to Zone 6. All of these hydrangea species have harder, more woody stems that cope better with frost and snow than the green, sappy stems of *H. macrophylla*. Snow can be a blessing in winter as it insulates plants from cold winds and frost. Generally, hydrangeas have a strong framework that is strong enough and flexible enough to avoid physical damage from snow. They also have the ability to produce flowers on the tips of their new spring growth, which means that even if the first batch of stems are killed by frost, the subsequent stems will still have flowers. If you live in a cold winter zone it may be best to choose from these species, which today provide an incredible array of cultivars.

Nearly all these hydrangeas come from mountain areas with lots of rain so they all prefer a moist soil and a regular supply of water through the summer months. While not as thirsty as the macrophyllas, they still need regular moisture because nearly all their roots are in the top foot or 12 in. (30 cm) of soil, and this is the first area of ground to dry out. Mulching will certainly help them remain in good condition as it reduces evaporation and keeps the roots cooler during the heat of summer and warmer in winter.

Hydrangea arborescens 'White Dome' in snow.

All prefer at least half a day of sun, or perhaps a little dappled shade in a woodland setting. *H. paniculata* is the best of all for full sun as it seems to cope, even with such large flowerheads, but as long as your summers are not too scorching most of these hydrangeas will handle full sun. However, being woodland plants by nature, they don't like buffeting winds. All of them have rather brittle stems. The heavy-headed *H. paniculata* types are especially prone to breaking and will snap easily in a storm. The rather stiff stems would probably cope with the wind were it not for the pressure produced by the very heavy flowers.

Choosing the ideal situation for hydrangeas in your garden depends very much on where you live. Is your garden hot and sunny? Perhaps you have some difficult shady areas. The annual rainfall is important, as is its cycle. Is it spread throughout the year or do you live in an area prone to droughts? If you are new to the region or inexperienced at gardening, talk to your neighbors or, better still, join a local gardening group. You'll find knowledgeable gardeners are very

Hydrangea macrophylla 'Red Star' grown in an acid soil.

keen to share their expertise. Other avenues of information are the local library, and your regional meteorological office will have records of rainfall and temperatures. Hopefully your local garden centers will also have knowledgeable staff to lead you in the right direction.

Soils and drainage

Hydrangeas are easy to please when it comes to soil as they will cope with almost any soil type and a wide range of acidity. Most other shrubs are much more demanding. Few woody plants grow well in limey, or alkaline, soils but hydrangeas cope quite well. As regards drainage, they would prefer to be in a loamy free-draining soil, but will manage better than most in poor soils. *H. macrophylla* is the most resilient in this regard, and plants are often found growing in heavy clay soils and even semi-swamp–like conditions.

It is possible to improve a poor soil. Some soils are impoverished and others suffer from poor drainage. We can improve both types by adding organic matter. In nature, the soil enjoys an annual dump of fallen leaves. As the soil fauna, such as worms, springtails, insect larvae, centipedes and microorganisms (fungi and bacteria), devour these fallen leaves they release nutrients that can be taken up by plants.

There is also a physical benefit because the organic matter helps to bind the soil particles, improving its structure and thus its drainage and aeration properties. We can imitate this yearly windfall by covering the soil with old leaves, compost and farm manure. Some people dig the organic matter into the ground, but this is not necessary as the soil fauna will do the job for you in a much more efficient way. There are different insects, larvae and so on at every level within the soil and when you dig the ground you turn their world literally upside down, killing many of them.

Take care when adding farm manures directly around plants as the high nitrogen levels can be toxic to the plant roots. Ideally farm manure should be placed in a compost bin for a few months before being used directly on your plants. Chicken manure is especially strong and dangerous in its raw form, but sheep, cattle and horse manures are all safer if composted first. It is often easier, and safer for your plants, to buy ready-composted manure from your local garden center. In a sandy soil the drainage is already very good, but the soil is usually impoverished. The organic matter will add nutrients to the soil and consequently your plants will be much healthier.

Improving soil drainage is one of the best things we can do for our gardens and our plants. Plant roots need air as much as they need water and if the soil remains sodden or waterlogged for long the plants will suffer and possibly die. We've all seen those sad-looking indoor plants in hard-packed potting mix. Repot them and they come back to life because the roots have air again. In the garden the same thing happens when soils are compacted. Some gardeners resort to digging trenches and laying drains to take away excess moisture, which is very expensive and tends to damage the soil structure. It is better to work with nature, adding compost and organic matter, and then letting the worms and soil fauna improve the structure and drainage.

Chemical fertilizers can be added to improve the fertility of a soil, but will not change the drainage in any way. The one exception to this rule is gypsum (calcium sulfate), which is a safe kind of lime that makes the soil particles clump together, thus improving the drainage. Heavy clay soils are made up of millions of tiny clay particles that stick together like glue, packing down the soil and preventing water from percolating through. Gypsum draws these clay particles together to form lumps and the increased space between these lumps allows more water and air to penetrate. Gardeners like gypsum because it is a form of lime acceptable to acid-loving plants such as rhododendrons, and because it does not change the pH of the soil. Another "safe" form of lime is dolomite lime, which has no influence on pH, but it has the added advantage of releasing magnesium, an essential plant element.

Soil acidity or alkalinity and its effects on *H. macrophylla*

All hydrangeas grow best in a slightly acid soil. Alkaline soils tend to lock up certain nutrients the plants need to keep their leaves green and lush, and too much lime will turn the leaves yellow.

Soil acidity has a remarkable effect on *H. macrophylla* flowers, making them change color. No other plant is affected by acidity in this way. In acid soils the

To achieve a scintillating blue, grow *Hydrangea macrophylla* 'Endiazom' (syn. 'Gentian Dome') in acid soil.

Even in an acid soil *Hydrangea macrophylla* 'Red Emperor' will try to stay red; in alkaline soil its flowers are a vivid crimson.

flowers will be blue and in alkaline or lime soils they are reds and pinks. In theory, we can change the soil to create the colors we want, but in reality it is quite difficult to change the pH of soil in the garden. It is much easier to manipulate the pH in tubs and pots to create the range of colors we desire.

Most gardeners think that if their soil is acid, their hydrangea flowers will be blue—or if alkaline, pink—but it is more complicated than that. The element that makes them go blue is aluminum, and it can take several years for the plant to accumulate enough aluminum to make the flowers blue. Often they are pink the first year of flowering, gradually changing from pink to mauve and finally to blue.

Why does this happen? Well, no one really knows why, but we do know how. Soil acidity is measured in pH units. A pH of 7 is neutral, neither acid or alkaline. Above 7 is alkaline and the higher the number, the more alkaline it is. Below 7 is acid and the lower the number, the more acid. The pH scale is a logarithmic scale, so pH 6 is ten times more acid than pH 7, pH 5 is therefore ten times more acid than pH 6. So pH 5 is therefore 100 times more acid than pH 7. Most soils are between 4.5, which is very acid, and 7.5, which is very alkaline and only found in limestone country. Yes, there are intermediates between each large number and thus 6.4 is more acid than 6.5. Remember we go down the scale for acid and for blue hydrangeas. There are pH test kits available from garden centers, if you want to measure the pH of your soil. To recap, acid soils = blue flowers for hydrangeas, and alkaline or lime soils = pink or red flowers. In reality pH 6.0 will give reasonable reds and pinks, even though this is slightly acid.

Sometimes it is possible to grow pink and blue varieties together, as in this roadside border.

Before you rush out and try to change your soil to acquire the brilliant blues or red flowers you have always wanted, take a moment to ponder why you want to make these changes. In my experience, gardeners always want what they cannot have. I know gardeners with alkaline soil who grow superb red hydrangeas, but are they satisfied? No, they want blue ones. They would willingly pay twice as much for the plant if you could "make" it blue. Likewise, people in acid-soil areas would give their eye-teeth for pinks and reds. Years of gardening experience have taught me to "go with nature" rather than try to fight it.

With the different colored hydrangeas, it is much easier to grow 'Nightingale' or 'Blaumeise' for fabulous blues in acid soil, and choose 'Fasan' and 'Zaunkönig' for splendid pinks and reds if you have alkaline soil. Many hydrangeas are wonderful whatever the soil. The whites are white, of course, wherever they are. The serrata types like 'Grayswood' and 'Preziosa' change from white to pink to red, regardless of the soil. Some macrophylla types like 'Merritt's Supreme' and 'Président Doumer' display wonderfully rich colors in any soil, though they will vary.

Fertilizing

A little slow-release fertilizer at planting time will help the plant become established. Thereafter a handful of general garden fertilizer every spring would help, but it's not essential.

H. macrophylla types are quite greedy plants and appreciate a spring application containing high nitrogen. If possible, spread the fertilizer before rain, so it will wash into the ground and be diluted. Apply any compost or well-rotted farm manure in spring to allow it to provide nutrients through the summer. No need to dig it in; let the worms and soil fauna break down the organic matter for you. Avoid feeding the plants in late summer as it only encourages soft growth that is at risk of being nipped by frost. Hydrangea plants do not need feeding in winter.

Feeding to get blue flowers

If you have acid soil you will be able to grow magnificent blue hydrangeas. If you or your neighbors can grow rhododendrons successfully, you can be confident you

TOP: *Hydrangea macrophylla* 'Forever' is soft shell-pink but in acid soil the flowers are smoky blue.

ABOVE: The flowers of *Hydrangea macrophylla* 'Dooley' are pink or blue, depending on your soil.

ABOVE RIGHT: *Hydrangea macrophylla* 'Blue Prince'

have acid soil. As mentioned already, hydrangeas may take up to three years to settle into a permanent color. You can speed up this process by feeding them aluminum sulfate. If you are keen to have blue hydrangeas, the process is as follows.

Potassium aluminum sulfate, sometimes called potash alum or just alum, is a very safe way of adding aluminum to give blue flowers. If you can't find it at your garden center, try your pharmacist.

Adding 9 oz per square yard (250 g per square meter) of aluminum sulfate will speed up the blueing process. It is free aluminum in the soil absorbed by the plant that turns the flowers blue. Beware, though—too much aluminum in one dollop can be dangerous to plant roots. "A little and often" is a good motto with this and other fertilizers.

Instead of sprinkling a year's worth of fertilizer on a plant in one go, with the risk of burning the roots or scorching the leaves, it is better to put on one-third of the annual amount three times a year. I know this adds to your workload, but it is much kinder to the plant. I try to remember to feed my plants two or three times a year, between early spring and mid to late summer. Feeding times depend on your climate. There is no point in feeding plants in midsummer if everything is in drought mode. Plants need water to absorb fertilizer and if the ground is too dry, this increases the concentration of fertilizer and thus the risk of damaging your plants. Fertilizer always works best with adequate rainfall or irrigation.

If you're growing hydrangeas in pots, you can add some aluminum sulfate to the surface of the potting mix in spring, say around ¾ to 1½ oz (20–40 g) for a 3 gal. (11 liter) pot. Remember "a little and often" is always the safer motto.

Plants need three major or macro- nutrients: nitrogen, phosphate (phosphorus) and potash (potassium) sometimes referred to by their chemical code N, P and K. On a bag of garden fertilizer it will give the NPK ratio to let you know what percentage of each is included. These macronutrients are needed to sustain plant growth and health. A general fertilizer for blue hydrangeas needs to be high in nitrogen and potash, and low in phosphates. Avoid superphosphate as this makes soil alkaline. A good NPK mix would be 25-5-30 ratio. Ideally the nitrogen should be in nitrate form rather than ammonium. Nitrates are released slowly to the plant whereas ammonium forms of nitrogen are quick acting and increase the risk of burning the roots.

Hydrangea macrophylla 'Gartenbaudirektor Kühnert' is not recommended for alkaline soils as its wonderful sky-blue flowers turn a muddy color.

Plants also need other nutrients, though in much smaller doses, and these are called micro- or trace elements. Elements such as copper and zinc are needed in minute quantities. Most soils naturally contain all these elements, including the NPK, but a top-up to improve the health of the plant is always beneficial. Natural fertilizers such as manure and compost contain some of these nutrients, too. Potting mixes should have these nutrients added, but do make sure before you buy.

The pH of the soil will affect the availability of various elements. Some elements become unavailable to the plant in high pH, or alkaline, soils. Calcium or lime tends to lock up certain plant nutrients, so while the soil may have all the essential nutrients, they may not be released to the plant. To counteract this you can add iron as iron sulfate at 1 oz per square yard (30 g per square meter). Iron negates the effects of lime and allows certain elements to be more readily available to plants.

BELOW: Hydrangea macrophylla 'Eternity'

BOTTOM: Hydrangea macrophylla 'Ami Pasquier' is one of the best crimson hydrangeas for alkaline soils and is also pretty in acidic soil.

Feeding to get pink and red flowers

Aluminum is unavailable to our plants in alkaline, or limey, soils. It is aluminum and not iron, as formerly believed, that makes hydrangea flowers turn blue. Iron plays a role in this by allowing aluminum to be available to the plant. This is because calcium and iron are antagonistic, so if you have too much calcium the iron doesn't work and therefore the aluminum doesn't work either.

In lime soils you can grow terrific red and pink hydrangeas, but you will struggle to grow good blues. Even if your soil is slightly acid, say a pH of 6.5, you will still grow good reds. In soils with a pH below 6 you will need to add lime to make your flowers turn red.

Adding lime twice a year in spring and again in summer will increase the pH. Be careful, as too much lime at one time can cause chlorosis, or leaf-yellowing. Also take care not to put lime too close to acid-loving plants such as rhododendrons. Perhaps an easier way to change the flowers to red is to add a fertilizer mix with plenty of phosphorus as this locks up aluminum and prevents the plant from accessing it. A fertilizer with an NPK ratio of 10-30-10 would be suitable.

Other ways to grow red hydrangeas

If you have acid soil and you're keen to grow pink and red hydrangeas there are other ways to do it. Perhaps the easiest method is to grow the plant in a tub or raised bed where the soil or potting mix can be altered to give red and pink flowers.

If your house has concrete foundations, or you have a concrete pathway, then you have a ready-made way of making the flowers red. The cement in the concrete contains lime. By planting your red and pink hydrangeas beside the concrete foundations they will immediately have access to more free calcium. You can add to this by feeding the plant with lime.

Another option is to select one portion of your garden for all the lime-loving plants and keep adding lots of lime until the hydrangea flowers gradually turn pink. This is unlikely to work if your soil is very acid. One area of most gardens that gets regular doses of lime is the vegetable garden as cabbages and other brassicas love lime. You could grow your red hydrangeas as a hedge or border next to the vegetable garden.

If you want only one or two red hydrangeas you could dig a large hole and line the sides with polyethylene. The hole should be at least 3 ft. wide by 3 ft. deep (1 m x 1 m). Do not put polyethylene in the bottom of the hole or the drainage will be impeded. Fill the hole with alkaline soil or potting mix. Because hydrangeas are fairly shallow-rooted, all the roots will be feeding in your alkaline mix and so the flowers will be pink or red.

If you want to grow pink and red hydrangeas and you have an acid soil, consider growing a suitably small variety in a container.

Ways to grow blue hydrangeas

The same schemes as above, such as growing plants in tubs or in a polyethylene-lined hole, will work—but remember, this time you need a potting mix laced with aluminum.

You will still need to feed with additional iron sulfate and aluminum sulfate every spring to keep good blues. Alum or aluminum sulfate can stunt the growth of young plants and so should be applied sparingly.

One other thing to be aware of is the water your plants receive. Tap water in a region of alkaline soils is likely to be "hard" lime water. Alkaline water is called "hard" and acid water is "soft." An easy way to tell what type of water you have is to look inside your electric jug or kettle. If the jug has a thick white deposit over the element and on the inner walls you have hard water. This deposit is made from lime crystals. For acid-loving blue hydrangeas you could collect rainwater in a barrel under your downspouts.

Mulches

Mulches are usually applied to suppress existing weeds and to prevent new weed seeds from germinating. Weed seeds need light to germinate and a layer of mulch will deny them the necessary sunlight. Mulches also help retain moisture in the soil by reducing evaporation and thus reduce the need to water. This is especially important for hydrangeas as they have most of their roots in the top few inches of soil, with only a few stronger roots going deeper to anchor the plant. If the topsoil dries out, the plants will suffer from drought stress because most of the roots are near the surface. There may be moisture further down, but the plant cannot reach it. You could install an expensive irrigation system to water your plants regularly to prevent the soil drying out, but a mulch can do the same job. It is also a much cheaper alternative with the added bonus of fewer weeds and, if you are in a drier region, better water conservation. Mulches also reduce temperature fluctuations in the soil, keeping it warmer in winter and cooler in summer.

A mulch has other benefits. It will gradually improve the soil structure, making the drainage better and encouraging root growth. Underneath the mulch, protected from the elements, will be a host of invisible organisms and soil fauna busily breaking down the organic matter to provide food for the plant roots. With their help fallen leaves will rot much more quickly, proving a more speedy return of nutrients to the soil.

Many gardeners now make their own mulch, using shredding machines to break down larger branches. All mulches will gradually rot down and this helps feed the soil, but be aware that a fresh mulch will rob the soil of nitrogen temporarily. The rotting process requires nitrogen and you should add a slow-acting nitrogen fertilizer to compensate for this. Some mulches take more nitrogen to break down. The biggest culprits are sawdust and straw, which will make your plants go yellow from lack of nitrogen if you don't apply any extra.

Ideally mulches should be open enough in structure to let water percolate through. Often it's a case of what is most readily available in your area. Be inventive—you can use waste from canning factories such as pea pods and peach stones. More commonly, mulches include tree bark or post peelings from sawmills. Make sure the wood peelings are not from treated timber as the dangerous preservatives used in the treatment process can kill your plants.

Watering

Hydrangeas planted in tubs, pots and raised beds will need regular watering. First find out the acidity of your water supply. Town water is often alkaline, which is fine for pinks and reds but not for blue *H. macrophylla*. Rainwater, which is generally slightly acidic, may be a better option for potted plants with blue flowers.

Hydrangeas in the author's garden provide splashes of color amid a variety of trees and shrubs.

Most hydrangea species like a moist soil and regular rainfall. *H. macrophylla* types are especially thirsty because of their big leaves and large flowerheads. If you live in an area of low rainfall, choose as moist a site as you can and be sure to use a mulch. If you still need to provide your hydrangeas with extra water, there are a few options. You can water your plants with a hose, but this is a slow process and is not always the most efficient way of getting maximum water to the roots. Sprinklers save time but can cause soil erosion and be wasteful of water, and the water droplets landing on the flowers and leaves can cause spotting and increase the likelihood of diseases.

Permanent trickle irrigation is the ideal solution. The water is delivered at ground level and slowly percolates into the soil and thus the roots are thoroughly watered. Trickle irrigation conserves moisture, as most of the water ends up in the ground rather than being lost by evaporation. Trickle irrigation systems are also relatively inexpensive to buy and use less water than other methods.

Plant selection

Hydrangeas are popular worldwide and are easy to find in plant shops and garden centers. Try not to buy plants on impulse, as they may not be ideal for your climate or your soil. It's very tempting to buy them when in flower and ignore the finer details about hardiness, height and color. Ideally, work out in advance which hydrangea species will do well in your area and then choose varieties that give the colors you want and grow to a height that fits the site. It's all too easy to plant the shrub and find out later it's going to block light to your windows or other garden plants. While most garden centers sell a range of hydrangeas, you may need to contact a specialist mail-order nursery if you want a greater range of varieties.

If you know which species and cultivars you want, it is simply a matter of choosing the best plant available. In summer, choose the plant with the best shape and healthy foliage. In winter, when there are no leaves, look for the best shape of plant.

Planting

When choosing the site for your plant, take care to select somewhere where the soil is acceptable, where there is space for the plant to grow and where there are suitable amounts of sun or shade.

When you are ready to plant, make sure the root ball of your hydrangea is thoroughly wet through by dropping the pot into a bucket of water until the bubbles stop, then lift and drain. Dig a hole deeper and wider than the pot and then fork the sides of the hole a little so the roots can more easily penetrate the surrounding soil.

If the plant is in a pot, first hold your fingers across the top of the pot and around the base of the stem. Then turn the pot upside down and tap gently until the plant and root ball fall away from the pot. Tease the roots out a little before placing the plant in the hole. The top surface of the potting mix should be level with the surrounding soil. Fill in the hole and maybe add a little slow-release general fertilizer and, if your soil is very poor, you could add some well-rotted compost. Then firm the soil around the plant using your heel for pressure, but don't pack it down too hard. Ideally you should surround the plant with a suitable mulch and then water well.

Some plants are sold wrapped in cloth or burlap, which should be removed before planting, but if the roots have grown through the material, it's better to plant the whole root ball. Just untie the cloth from around the stem and the rest of it will rot away in time.

Sometimes we discover a plant is not in the best position. It may be too big for the site, or in too sunny or shady a spot. You can shift hydrangeas during winter without too much risk. Prune the plant back and then dig it up and shift into the new site immediately. If your plant is a *H. macrophylla* it will change color to pink or red after the shift because it has lost access to aluminum.

Pruning, Pests and Propagation

Pruning hydrangeas

Not all hydrangeas need pruning; some species will grow and flower quite happily every year without ever needing any shaping. Even the *Hydrangea macrophylla* types will still perform well and produce multiple flowers if you forget to prune them. In fact, the plant will produce even more flowers than the previous season, but they will be smaller. In the wild, a plant never gets pruned and so we have invented pruning regimes to make a plant tidier or to produce bigger flowers.

It is worth considering just why we prune shrubs.

We prune:

1 for the health of the plant by removing any dead and diseased wood. Do this before any other pruning so you know what is left to prune.

2 to improve the shape of the bush; to make it tidier or to open it up and allow in more light and air— this improves the health of the plant. Often the critical time for this type of pruning is in the plant's early years when you can prune to create a balanced shape.

3 to increase the number of flowers. In some cases, such as *H. macrophylla*, pruning is done to decrease the total number of flowers, but in doing so the size is increased as is the quality.

OPPOSITE: If your hydrangea is growing in a formal setting, you will need to prune it to help keep its shape.

RIGHT: Pruning can help to create a mass display of good-sized flowers.

ABOVE: Pruning to the lowest set of flower buds will increase the size of the flowerheads. If not pruned in this way, your hydrangea will produce more flowers of smaller size.

ABOVE RIGHT: The swelling flower buds are easy to see in this photograph.

Most garden shrubs should be pruned immediately after flowering, giving the plant a whole year to produce strong new growth for next year's flowers. Hydrangeas are one of the few exceptions to this rule and are best pruned in winter, or at the very end of the winter if your area is prone to late frosts.

The pruning routine for popular varieties

Apart from an occasional tidy-up, the wild forms of *H. arborescens* do not need any pruning. For the cultivated forms of *H. arborescens* like 'Annabelle' and 'Grandiflora' there are a few options. One is to lightly shear off the dead flowers in winter. Another is a light pruning, removing say one-third to one-half of last summer's growth, resulting in a tidy bush with modest-sized flowers.

The other pruning method is more drastic and involves cutting all the stems to ground level. The bush responds by sending up strong stems with much larger flowerheads because of the increased vigor of the new growth. This technique is feasible only because this species produces flowers at the tips of the new spring growth.

H. aspera subsp. villosa and H. heteromalla do not need any pruning apart from an occasional tidy-up, and will not suffer in the least if they are never pruned. You may wish to remove the dead flowerheads at some time and it is probably a good idea to prune them for shape in the early years. A light pruning at this stage can be very useful, but beware of over-vigorous pruning because it will delay the establishment of the bush.

For *H. quercifolia* it is a good idea to remove the spent flowerheads as they are so large and look untidy in winter. In general, *H. quercifolia* does not need any further attention, other than pruning for shape or size.

H. paniculata species can be left unpruned like those above, and this is probably the best course of action for 'Kyushu' and 'Praecox'.

For the larger-blooming types such as 'Grandiflora' there are two pruning styles depending on whether you want medium or giant flowerheads. If you don't like enormous heads, you can prune lightly and you will have more flowers, but each one will be smaller. If you want bigger heads then prune hard. The more drastic the pruning, the more vigorous the new growth. You can invigorate the plant by cutting the previous summer's growth back really hard to one or two buds, leaving just 1–2 in. (3–4 cm) of last summer's growth.

A popular method of pruning *H. paniculata* 'Grandiflora' is to establish a short main trunk on the plant over the first few years of growth, then keep this as the only permanent part of the plant. Every winter the long flower stems of the previous summer are cut back hard to one or two buds. From these buds strong new growth will appear in the spring and give rise to the gigantic blooms that make these peegee hydrangeas so famous. If you choose not to prune, the plant will grow more flower stems and subsequently all the

ABOVE: **Hydrangea serrata** 'Kiyosumi' (left) can be left unpruned, but smaller flowers and a more untidy shrub will be the result. **Hydrangea paniculata** 'Praecox' (right), on the other hand, is best left unpruned.

flowerheads will be smaller because of the increased competition for nutrients and water.

Pruning macrophylla and serrata types

There are basically two types of flowers on *H. macrophylla* and *H. serrata* cultivars: the big round mopheads and the flatter lacecaps. In winter the big, brown, parchment-like heads on the mops can look untidy, whereas the heads of a lacecap will hardly be noticed. Both types need pruning if you want to have a tidy bush with plenty of robust flowers the next season.

If your hydrangeas are blue, the papery flowerheads will contain a high level of aluminum (the chemical that turns them blue). It is a shame to waste this readily accessible aluminum by trimming them off. Why not recycle this aluminum by pushing the pruned heads back in under the bush? You may need to weigh them down with a log until they start to rot, otherwise they may blow around the garden like tumbleweeds.

They will not, however, suffer unduly if left unpruned. All that happens is that the new growth will emerge and completely cover the old dead heads. The resulting flowers on the tips will be smaller because the bush has the maximum number of flowers. When you prune you will reduce the number of flower buds, and thus the number of flowers. Fewer flowers mean bigger heads because each one has less competition for nutrients and more energy and vigor as a result.

Year one, a young plant produces a flower at the tip of each stem. Year two, it produces two flower shoots from side growths of this first stem. The number of shoots with flowers on from this original base stem will build up each year to 20 or so flowers.

There are several methods of pruning you can use for *macrophylla* and serrata types.

1 You can thin the whole bush, allowing in more light and air. Eventually the wood in the center of the plant gets old and exhausted. What I recommend on a large established bush is to cut out two or three entire old stems from as near to the base as you can. This has the effect of thinning the bush and reducing overcrowding. The plant will have fewer but bigger flowers next year, as there is less competition. Do this annual thinning every year in late winter or spring, depending on your climate and the likelihood of late frosts. You can trim the tops of the remaining stems if you want bigger blooms next summer.

2 Keep the bushes at a reasonable height and have a good display of flowers every summer. In this case you can prune lightly overall instead of just removing the dead flowerheads. Look for the large buds; these are next summer's flowers. They are usually in opposite pairs near the tops of the stems. You need to retain as many of the fat flower buds

as is practicable for the bush to flower well. Thin the stems, at the same time removing the weaker growths, then reduce the height of the remaining stems, remembering to preserve enough flower buds.

3 Prune the bush to increase the size of the flowerheads. This method will increase the individual size of the blooms at the expense of the overall display, i.e., the bush will have fewer flowers, but each will be larger. First, remove all the thin and spindly growths, generally cutting these out as low as you can go. You are now left with good, robust stems. The next task is to prune these strong stems. Holding a stem in one hand and pruning shears in the other, go down the stem until you find the lowest set of big buds. These fat flowering buds are found only on *H. macrophylla* and *H. serrata*, but in the latter they tend to be thinner and more pointed. Other species of hydrangeas produce flowers on new summer growth so there are no overwintering flower buds.

Remove dead flowerheads and trim the bush to shape for a tidier-looking hydrangea (see the plant at the back).

What do these big buds look like? Near the tops of the stem there will be fat buds the size of a fingernail, usually in pairs with one on either side of the stem. Occasionally there is only one fat bud with a tiny bud on the opposite side. The buds below these down to the center of the bush will be smaller buds—these are growth buds.

Each fat bud contains a new stem and a flowerhead in miniature. If a stem has six fat buds, it will produce six small flowerheads during the summer and may therefore be rather crowded. Pruning back to leave just one fat bud, or maybe one pair of buds, will give the large blooms we appreciate. Do this to all the stems and it is likely that you will be left with 15 to 25 fat flower buds for next summer's display.

Some *H. macrophylla* and *H. serrata* bushes will produce flowers from the tiny growth buds, but these flowers generally appear later in the summer. The varieties capable of flowering from growth buds are especially important in cold regions where the flower buds are frosted and killed every winter. In warm Zone 9 and 10 regions it seems that virtually all hydrangeas are remontant (blooming more than once in a year). If you prune drastically, you are forcing the plant to be remontant and this will delay the flowering in the following summer as the severe pruning will probably remove all the fat flower buds and the bush will have to make flowers from the growth buds.

Make your cuts flat, at 90 degrees to the stem, and prune to just above the buds. Prune too high and the stem is inclined to die back. Luckily, this is not a major problem with hydrangeas, unlike some shrubs, such as roses, which demand more accurate pruning to prevent dieback and subsequent disease infections.

RIGHT: Spider mites can cause distortion of the leaves.

BELOW: A layer of mulch, pine needles, or other rough organic matter will deter slugs and snails from attacking your newly planted shrubs.

Climbing hydrangeas

These should not need any pruning other than to keep their shape. If you have a hydrangea growing up a house wall, then obviously you are going to have to prune it around the perimeter of the windows. Tidy gardeners may want to remove the spent flowerheads, but these usually disappear over winter.

Pests and diseases

Hydrangeas really are easy-care plants and part of the reason for this is that they are little troubled by pests or diseases. In 20 years I have never had cause to spray the hydrangeas in my garden for any pests or diseases. The following is a sample of the most likely pests you may encounter.

Slugs and snails

Slugs and snails can be a problem especially on the *H. macrophylla* types and they have a special liking for the variegated cultivars. On a small, recently planted bush they can devour all the emerging buds, and if they keep munching the new growth the plant will eventually die. A layer of pine needles or sawdust around your newly planted shrubs will deter them. You can use slug bait, but there is a danger of hurting your pets or native birds. I still remember the stress of seeing our sick Labrador after she ate slug pellets. There are more environmentally appropriate ways of reducing slug numbers. They love beer, so a small dish or tin of beer in the garden will draw them from a wide area. The slugs then drown in the beer. If you're not a beer drinker, you could toss out pieces of orange peel or slices of uncooked potato. The next morning you'll find slugs and snails have attached themselves to the moist surfaces and you can dispose of them before throwing the bait back onto the garden to catch more slugs.

Deer

Deer can be a major problem for gardeners. They seem to love all the plants that we do, the only difference being they eat them instead of admiring them. Fencing to exclude deer is very expensive and often rather unsightly, but it may be essential if the problem persists. Deterrent sprays work for some gardeners but not others.

Thrips

Thrips can be a pest in warm climates, say Zones 9 and 10, and also on hydrangeas as house plants. These tiny narrow creatures are about the size of a pinhead. The juveniles are creamy-yellow and the adults black. You will realize they are present if the top surface of the leaves turns silver or if you see a muddy stain on the underside of the leaves. In the garden, thrips like to be in shady places and usually choose the inside or shady part of the plant. Any insecticide used on roses will kill them. On house plants, a regular misting of water will deter them as they like to be hot and dry. If your hydrangeas are near the house you could occasionally blast them with the hose to keep thrips at bay.

Spider mites

Spider mites are like thrips in that they love warm, dry locations. They usually attack only hydrangeas grown indoors or in conservatories, or in very warm climates. The first sign of them is a very fine webbing on the leaves. Later the leaves may become distorted and pale. For a minor attack, remove and burn badly affected leaves, then blast the plant with water from the hose. Like thrips, mites hate frequent moisture, so an occasional blast with the hose, or misting your house plant with a spray of water once or twice a week, will both freshen up your hydrangeas and deter the mites.

Another spider mite called *Eriophyid* mite can distort the new stems and leaves on *H. macrophylla* and give the appearance of a virus attack.

Mildew can be a problem in shady sites.

Botrytis

Botrytis is often a problem late in summer especially in a wet or humid climate. It's basically a common rot fungus that needs a moist atmosphere to attack plants and fruit. It first appears as a gray mold—like off-white fluff—and then gradually spreads. It's more likely to be seen on flowers than on leaves, and often appears after a period of heavy rain. The disease is always present, but needs a wound to infect a plant and often attacks the flowers after they have been sunburned. You can reduce the risk of disease by good hygiene. Remove any dead leaves and spent flowers and prune off any dead and dying parts of the plant. Young plants and seedlings are more prone to this disease as they don't have the robust strength of older plants. Usually the disease is not bad enough to need spraying, but should it get too bad you can use a rose spray. There are new products using the friendly fungus *Trichoderma* to prevent botrytis becoming established. These "good guy" fungi muscle out the baddies.

Mildew

This disease is mainly a problem on plants grown indoors. It can also occur on plants in the garden, especially in humid regions, appearing in late summer and usually on plants that are under stress. Mildew is usually worse in shady sites. When the infestation is severe, there are little patches of dead cell regions in the leaf. The best way to keep it at bay is by having healthy plants. Regular feeding, mulching and watering will reduce mildew attacks. If the problem is severe, an all-purpose rose spray will fix it. Some cultivars are especially prone to mildew and it pays to avoid or discard these ones.

Root rots

Root rots can be a problem for *H. arborescens* and *H. quercifolia*. The most likely cause is *Phytophthora* disease, which is encouraged by wet soil and humid atmospheric conditions. Either improve the drainage or move the plant to a more free-draining area. Fungicides may help prevent or cure the problem. Another option is to spray a foliar phosphate solution. This increases the health of the plant and helps keep the disease in check.

Armillaria

This devastating fungus sometimes known as mushroom root rot attacks the roots of many trees and shrubs, usually infecting a dead tree and then spreading to other nearby shrubs. Sometimes called the bootlace fungus because of the underground threads found spreading from tree to tree, above ground the only signs are honey-colored toadstools. If you cut out a tree, the roots remain alive but stressed, and this is when the fungus is likely to invade and feed off the roots as a parasite. The disease is more likely to attack a weak plant than vigorous healthy plants. Keeping your plants well fed, mulched and watered will help prevent this problem.

Wilting

When your plants are wilting it could be disease, but it may just be stress caused by heat and lack of moisture. So if your plants wilt in the heat of summer, the most likely cause will be heat stress. For *H. macrophylla* types this can be devastating as the blooms will collapse and the flowers may die, leaving you with ugly brown heads. If possible, place a hose by the roots, turn the tap on very slightly and let a tiny trickle of water soak your plant over several hours. For a long-term solution, add a mulch around the roots to conserve moisture, and perhaps install some permanent irrigation if this is likely to be an ongoing problem. Alternatively, you can move the plant next winter to a damper site. If a drink of water doesn't solve the problem and your plant does not revive in the next few hours, then the most likely cause is a root rot. You will be guided by recent weather events. If it's been very dry weather, then it's probably lack of water. If you've had heavy rain, it's much more likely to be a root rot problem.

Leaf spots

There are some fungi, including *Anthracnose*, that can cause brown spots on the leaves. They are more likely to occur if your plants are stressed, so improving the drainage and adding mulches to keep the roots moist but not too wet will deter the fungi.

Chlorosis is caused by an inability to extract iron and other micronutrients from the soil.

Chlorosis

Chlorosis is not a disease but a lack of certain minerals and nutrients. This condition is often found with plants growing in lime, or alkaline, soils. They are unable to take up enough iron and other micronutrients because the calcium in the soil locks them up and makes them unavailable. Apply sulfate of iron to remedy the problem and lower the pH of the soil (it makes it more acidic), making the iron more readily available to the plant. Beware of tap water, which can be highly alkaline in certain regions.

Cold damage and frosts

Frosts can kill the buds on *H. macrophylla* hybrids and this is especially true on young, recently planted shrubs. On a mature plant, this probably means all your flower buds have been killed and you may not get any flowers next summer. On a young plant it can be even more devastating, as the plant may die. Remove any frosted buds that have a burned appearance, then gently prune back to clean, healthy wood, just above a bud. The combination of frosted buds and subsequent infections of botrytis can kill a young plant. Frequently a young plant suffers this problem in winter and is finally killed off by slugs eating the soft new growth in spring. Carefully select your site before planting and then keep an eye on your newly planted hydrangeas.

Sun scorch

This is related to the wilting problem. When your plant wilts the flowers will collapse. If the plant suffers from lack of water for too long the flowers will dry and get sun scorch, which turns the sepals brown. This effectively ruins the flower for the rest of the season and spoils an attractive head.

Viruses

Thankfully viruses are very rarely seen in hydrangeas. Typical symptoms are a narrowing and slight twisting of the leaves and also lengthways opaque streaks in the leaf. Once a plant has a virus, it is impossible to cure. There are no sprays or other remedies because the virus is in the sap stream of the plant and impossible to eradicate. The only safe thing to do is dig up and burn the plant before the virus attacks any other hydrangeas. Viruses are spread by sap-sucking insects such as aphids. If you think you have a virus problem and you're about to destroy the plant, check first that it's not *Eriophyid* mite causing the distortion.

Propagation

Hydrangeas are easy to propagate. If your friend has a plant you admire or you want to grow more of a certain hydrangea in your garden, it's usually easy enough to remove some cuttings. Ideally the cuttings should be around 4 in. (10 cm) long and from new growth not old wood. Take off the lower leaves and then make a cut just below a node where the buds and leaves emerge. Place your cuttings in a suitable potting mix and keep them moist. You can do this by covering them with a clear polyethylene bag or an inverted plastic bottle. *H. macrophylla* and *H. serrata* types are especially easy to propagate from cuttings. Some of the species types can be a bit trickier, but will root most times.

As a backup method you could try layering some stems. The easiest way to do this is pull a low branch down near the ground and place a brick over the stem to hold it down against the soil. Make sure there is enough of the stem tip, say 8–12 in. (20–30 cm), showing on the far side of the brick. The added moisture under the brick will encourage rooting. Leave it alone for a whole year, by which time you should have a new plant ready to separate from the parent plant. Remove rooted layers only in winter when the plant is dormant. Removing and transplanting the layer in summer may kill it.

Some of the species will send up suckers from around the base of the plant and these can be detached and grown as a new plant. This is a good way of making new plants of *H. arborescens* and *H. quercifolia*. If you crawl around the base of an old *H. macrophylla* you will likely find the plant has already rooted down where low branches have touched the ground. Remove these in winter for an instant new plant.

Landscaping with Hydrangeas

While we all like to have a variety of plants in our patch, it's possible to create a stunning garden using predominantly hydrangeas. A typical hydrangea grows 3–6 ft. (1–2 m) high and wide; this includes the macrophylla and serrata types, *Hydrangea quercifolia* and most *H. paniculata* types. There are some genuine dwarfs—plants around knee height—in all these groups for those of you with really small gardens. If your outdoor living space is made up of paving or decking, you can grow the smaller *H. macrophylla* types in pots and tubs. In many cities around the world these same varieties are used for summer-long color indoors and then discarded at the onset of winter.

Perfect settings for *H. arborescens*

You might imagine these hydrangeas, being a woodland plant, prefer dappled light, but while they do cope well with shade you will probably have healthier plants with more blooms if you grow them in full sun. This species is surprisingly drought tolerant and possibly the best choice if you want hydrangeas in a hot, dryish spot. As a general rule, the hotter your climate, the more shade they need.

Being white flowered, *H. arborescens* varieties blend with just about any garden plants. You can include them in a bed of mixed shrubs. They look just as good mingling in a herbaceous border or planted as a backdrop for perennial

OPPOSITE AND RIGHT:
The lush foliage and bold flowerheads of macrophylla hydrangeas make them popular choices for a strong entranceway.

Hydrangea aspera subsp. *villosa* is the most common *aspera* in cultivation.

flowers. The taller, wild types with the lacecap blossoms are probably best used at the back of a border as they can grow to 10 ft. (3 m) or more. The mopheaded 'Annabelle' and 'Grandiflora' types often arch over due to the weight of the blooms. These heavy-headed types are very effective in mixed borders and if you want to make a real show, plant a group of three or five under a cherry tree or similar deciduous specimen.

Effective sites for *H. aspera* species

This group of plants gathered around one species name can vary considerably so it pays to buy a good form from a known source. The most common type in cultivation is *H. a.* subsp. *villosa*, which has large pink sepals making up the outer ring of the lacecap and bluish-purple true flowers in the center. The contrast between the pink and purple is very pleasing. Because they grow 9–13 ft. (3–4 m) high, these really need to be seen from a distance and are probably best situated at the back of a mixed or herbaceous border. An even taller backdrop, such as a wall, fence or high hedge, will accentuate their beauty.

If you happen to have a sloping garden, put *H. aspera* shrubs near the bottom of the slope so you can look down on the flowers. The latter are easier to see if they have a dark backdrop rather than being silhouetted against a bright sky. These plants do cope with all-day sun, at least in cooler regions; it might pay to give them dappled light or only half-day sun in hotter areas. The leaves are narrow, hairy and not especially attractive.

There is an outstanding variant called *H. a.* subsp. *sargentiana* with huge, crispy, hairy leaves. Worth growing just for the foliage, this lush shrub really needs dappled light and is the perfect woodland plant in a rare-plant collection. To be grown successfully it needs to be in shade to protect the big leaves from damaging winds and hot sun. Ideally a mulch of well-rotted leaves or compost on the soil surface will keep the roots moist, though it does like good drainage. Plant it at the back of a border under the shade of something tall and lacy such as a maple.

H. heteromalla is very similar to *H. aspera* as a garden plant, with the same growing and site preferences.

H. macrophylla in the home landscape

While these fabulous plants will grow almost anywhere, they do still have preferences and can be used to better effect if we give a few moments' thought to their placement. In small gardens they are perfect as a statement plant next to an entrance, a door, a path and so on. They're ideal if you want a formal plant, on either side of an entrance, for example. Even if it's a paved yard, you can still have hydrangeas in large containers to accentuate the entranceways. Modest-sized varieties are ideal for planting under windows where you have a height restriction.

H. *macrophylla* is moisture loving and thrives beside water features in the small garden as well as next to streams, ponds and lakes in the wider landscape.

Unlike many less robust shrubs, *H. macrophylla* specimens become solid and substantial plants, brilliant in isolation. Because of their neat rounded appearance and equally neat and tidy blooms, they look perfect set against a wall, fence or hedge. Somehow the solid background accentuates their tidiness. Their bold leaves and dense habit also give the appearance of having more weight at the base and convey a grounded impression. If you have a confined yard or a deck, or a car-parking area where it's difficult to grow plants that look attractive for long periods as well as being tidy all year, hydrangeas could be the answer. If you grow a climbing rose on the wall behind as a color contrast, the effect will be even more stunning.

When planting a row of *H. macrophylla* along a fence line, you can use all the same color or create some variety by selecting different shades and heights, perhaps even choosing a mix of mopheads and lacecaps to make it more interesting. While these shrubs look good against a solid wooden fence, they're even more appealing when presenting their blooms through a picket fence. (Remember the advantage of the mophead hydrangeas over lacecaps is that they will be in flower for at least three months and possibly as long as six months, depending on your climate and watering regime.)

These macrophyllas make a brilliant poolside border and are neatly contained by a low boxwood hedge.

Macrophyllas are ideal for public spaces, as they are easy to grow and maintain.

Often we're stuck for something to grow in the shade; perhaps on the cool side of the house or else under a group of trees or beside the neighbors' hedge. Shrubs of *H. macrophylla* thrive in shade and will cope with all these situations. They will light up the sunless side of your house and bring drama to a shady woodland. White mopheads or lacecaps are best for brightening a dark part of your garden. Most shrubs wouldn't even survive these shady conditions and yet the hydrangeas will sparkle here. Another perfect spot to grow them is under trees at the far end of a lawn vista. All your visitors will be naturally drawn to this mass of color. And at the end of summer these lovely round heads will change to yet another color, creating a new scene for everyone to admire.

Amenity plantings

One rather neglected opportunity for using *H. macrophylla* is in our city parks and other public places, as well as industrial sites. Because they are so easy to grow and maintain, I feel that hydrangeas, especially *H. macrophylla*, could be used more in school grounds, at camping sites, around factories and in cemeteries. Amenity plantings in such locations require tough, long-flowering shrubs, especially varieties that peak in summer. Spring-flowering shrubs are common in parks and gardens, yet spring is a season of low visitor numbers because of the cooler weather. People visit parks in summer when the weather is more inviting, and I believe city parks departments could make much better use of low-maintenance hydrangeas for attractive displays in warmer months at minimal expense. They can be grown singly in a bed or used in groups for splashes of bold color.

In school grounds the caretaker does not have the time to cultivate large flower beds, and the risk of damage from children's ball games would make this a thankless task. Shrubs such as roses have thorns and need constant spraying with chemicals we would rather keep away from our children, so the resilient, easy-care hydrangea would seem ideal for such locations.

Even tough sites such as roadside planting, car parks and borders in front of industrial or office buildings would be suitable settings for hardy hydrangeas as they cope with all weathers and flower for months rather than days. Should they be damaged or vandalized, they will quickly recover. The fact they get so few pests and diseases also helps in these situations, as the plants can be left to their own devices without the need for spraying.

Color considerations

Color is important with macrophylla hydrangeas, the more so because they come in such an eye-catching range of white, pinks, reds, purples and blues.

The white cultivars are invaluable. White flowers have a tendency to burn in strong summer sun, but as white is such a highlight in a shady area, let's use this to our advantage. A group of white mopheads will lift even the gloomiest woodland garden. Similarly a white lacecap bush will appear as though it was made for a shady dell. The white lacecaps are less likely to burn in full sun as they don't need as much water as the mopheads. It isn't just the sunlight causing them to scorch; the plant loses moisture during the heat of the day and the flowers

Hardy hydrangeas are a perfect backdrop for a roadside picnic area.

wilt for a time, usually to be resuscitated at sunset. If the flower remains wilted for too long, the cells inside the petals will collapse, turning them an ugly brown.

Pink mopheads look great against a painted fence or a brick wall. Note that if the background color is too pale or too strong, the pink hues disappear. Reds are perfect against the rich greens of either shrubs or lawn. Dark blues look good almost anywhere—against a white picket fence, a red brick wall or in a host of other situations. Gardeners crave real blue flowers and, surprisingly, these seem to blend in most situations. Pale blues are similarly popular. Strangely enough, nearly all the pale blue varieties are rather delicate. That doesn't make them any less desirable. You just need to pick your planting spot a bit more carefully. 'Générale Vicomtesse de Vibraye', 'Nikko Blue' and 'Madame Truffaut' are the best and all look fantastic in a dell or under deciduous trees. Match them up with some of the whites for a refined or subtle contrast.

Good companions for *H. macrophylla*

Hydrangea macrophylla 'Générale Vicomtesse de Vibraye' in a colorful garden border with day lilies (*Hemerocallis*) in front.

Many different plants can be grown alongside hydrangeas to enhance a garden's overall design. However, because the majority of shrubs are spring flowering, there are relatively few that offer blossoms that could blend with hydrangeas, so most shrubs will only give a foliage backcloth. On the other hand, herbaceous

perennials blend extremely well with hydrangeas, especially *H. macrophylla* varieties. The latter's tidy shape, bold leaves and eye-catching blooms make them a perfect fit in summer mixed borders. The mopheads will be featured most effectively in a herbaceous border if you place them according to height, short ones near the front and large ones at the back. The lacecap types look better at the back of a bed or border because their flat-topped flowers somehow signal a visual end point.

In a shady border, hostas are ideal companions because their leaf mirrors the hydrangea leaf as a big bold heart shape and this gives continuity. You can match green with green or go for contrasts, using blue- and gray-foliaged hostas or even variegated ones. In sites getting a bit more sun, day lilies or *Hemerocallis* are wonderful too, because they begin flowering just before the hydrangea blooms emerge and carry on as a clever color contrast. The strap-like leaves of the day lilies contrast nicely with the bolder hydrangea leaves. Day lilies come in such a wonderful range of colors the combination possibilities are endless. You can use their subtle pastel colors with hydrangeas of rich blue and red, while the day lilies' intense reds and vivid golds are stupendous with opulent blue mopheads.

Astilbes are bold summer-flowering plants and can look stunning in drifts, especially when planted in tandem with hydrangeas. Likewise drifts of *Lobelia cardinalis* and *L. fulgens* cultivars offer those same contrasting spire-like flowers. Ligularias are a perfect foil for blue hydrangeas. Their gleaming gold and yellow daisy flowers will enhance the blues, and their rounded or kidney-shaped leaves blend easily with the bold macrophylla leaves.

All of the above-mentioned plants thrive in the moist conditions enjoyed by *H. macrophylla*, making the job of landscaping even easier. If your soil is a little drier, include the bright yellow solidago with blue mopheads. Cool clear-blue campanulas also complement white and blue hydrangeas and sometimes the bolder reds. To blend with reds and white you could try monarda and phlox.

For low-growing fillers and ground covers around hydrangeas, my favorites are the bright blue-flowered ajuga, which has the added attraction of shiny dark green or bronze leaves. Big bold-leaved bergenias are another possibility. Their pink flowers blend well with pink and white hydrangeas. *Alchemilla mollis*, whose fascinating leaves hold water droplets like mercury, are perfect with blue hydrangeas because of their fluffy yellow flowers. Penstemons are another possibility as a companion plant in borders.

Later in summer when the hydrangea heads change color we have to choose carefully so as not to clash with these new tones. Monardas with their rich reds and mauves are a good choice to team with red and white hydrangeas, while plants from the yellow daisy family—for example, rudbeckia—are very suitable for the blues and wine-reds. If your hydrangeas are in pots, you could grow geraniums nearby to good effect.

Using *H. paniculata* in the garden

H. paniculata should be in full sun or at least receive plenty of light. A reasonable amount of moisture is needed to keep the large blooms supplied with water, especially the huge peegee flowers. Having said that, this species is more drought tolerant than other hydrangeas. As with most hydrangeas, the hotter the summers, the more need for some dappled shade.

In general, plants of *H. paniculata* are easy to grow as they tolerate a range of soils as long as the drainage is reasonable. Their greatest asset is that they are very cold hardy and thus can be grown successfully in most regions. They are also reliable bloomers as they form their flower buds in spring on the tips of the new growth, so cold winters won't spoil their display. If they have a fault or two, it is that they can grow too big for small gardens, though you can prune them drastically to reduce their size. Another possible fault is that the blooms can be so heavy they bend or even break the stems.

Most of the lightweight flowerheads point skyward, but the very heavy 'Grandiflora' or peegee hydrangeas tend to arch out from the center, or even hang down with the weight of their blossoms. Planting them next to other weeping plants creates a harmonious effect. If you want to introduce some drama, choose a strong-colored weeping plant such as bronzy clones of *Acer palmatum*—for example, 'Red Dragon' or 'Crimson Queen'. The taller or more upright forms of *H. paniculata* also look fantastic situated beside these bronze maples, creating a garden picture no one can resist.

Hydrangea paniculata 'Burgundy lace'

Shrubs of *H. paniculata* blend very well with a wide variety of foliage plants, everything from bronze Japanese maples to simple green shrubs like box or rhododendron. Choosing a strong but low-key color seems to set the white frothy flowers alight, and a background of any dense shrub will enhance both *H. paniculata* flowers and the shape of its bush.

Another good site for a peegee hydrangea is right next to your house wall on the sunny side. Depending on the color of your walls, you can have a wonderful contrast. Naturally, being pure white, the flowers also look stunning against a grass green backdrop and so using lawn grass as the foreground and bright green shrubs as the background is perfect. Choose a spring-flowering shrub such as *Forsythia* or, even better, a *Philadelphus* as the backdrop. A seemingly boring summer shrub then has added value by providing a contrasting color.

H. paniculata types look good in a mixed border with herbaceous summer-flowering perennials. Adding extra height is just one advantage, and the airy, white, long-lasting blossoms blend easily with any colorful perennial flowers. Even the more solid-looking peegee hydrangeas look okay with perennials or

in a mixed shrub border. However, I think the peegees are so stunning they look best in isolation or surrounded by foliage rather than bright colors.

If you have a large garden, an avenue or border of *H. paniculata* will look amazing. Do try and choose a site with plenty of sunlight and somewhere without too much wind, remembering the brittle stems.

H. paniculata shrubs are often sparse near the base and you may want to consider some low-growing or ground-covering plants underneath them. Hostas are one possibility, but you may lose the finer points of the hosta structure as the hydrangea arches out over them. Mondo grass is probably a better bet as it remains short and dense and has the advantage of being ever-green. Dwarf azaleas such as the Gumpo series are ideal as they remain low and will help extend the color seasons in your garden. The azaleas will have the scene all to themselves during spring when the hydrangeas have no leaves and then it becomes a natural progression of flowering.

Often underestimated is the impact of the antique color of the late summer flowers. Some of the larger, denser flowerheads turn a lovely shade of pink and this can be a welcome addition to the surrounding fall colors.

H. quercifolia—good value in the garden

Like most other hydrangeas, these too are influenced by climate. In hot summer regions the plants do best in partial shade because they get too stressed with the heat, whereas in cooler, moist climates they thrive in full sun. If you're lucky enough to be able to grow *H. quercifolia* in full sun the bush will be tidier; a neat dome of foliage and flowers. In shade the plants are often rather ragged looking.

Shrubs of *H. quercifolia* are good value because they provide two or even three displays each summer. First they are blessed with big creamy cones of flowers in mid-season. These flowerheads last a remarkably long time and then as the cool nights of fall approach the blooms take on a lovely pink tinge. This is the time to pick them if you want to use them for dried flowers. As a stunning finale, the leaves turn a rich burgundy-purple and this contrasts brilliantly with the pinky shades in the fall flowers. Trying to find colors to match all of these hues is difficult. Perhaps it's easier to surround them in simple green. I have tried a low artemisia with silver foliage to create a stunning contrast with the burgundy fall colors, but it doesn't do much for the summer flowers. If you want a splendid contrast for the flowers, try highlighting them with a purple-leaved ajuga nearby.

Ideally you need plenty of space to grow these lovely plants because they tend to sprawl. The outline of *H. quercifolia* looks quite tidy, but each year you will find it takes up more and more space, so if you plant one near a path or lawn edge it will soon encroach, leaving you with no choice but to trim the shrub and lose some of its appeal.

Companion plants

Most of the suggestions for companion plants for *H. macrophylla* given on page 64 will work with the other hydrangeas discussed above. Bear in mind that most hydrangeas have white summer flowers, possibly changing to pink or reddish tones in fall. The yellow-flowered perennials won't work with these shrubs but the pinks and reds will be fine, as will most of the more subtle-toned campanulas and day lilies. Monardas look fetching next to the pink hues of *H. paniculata* and *H. quercifolia* cultivars. To blend with pink *H. aspera*, try pink or white cultivars of *Anemone hupehensis*. In fact, these will also work well with pink-hued *H. paniculata* and *H. quercifolia* cultivars.

Best sites for *H. serrata*

Although they look very similar to varieties of *H. macrophylla*, these plants are a bit more delicate and it's worth spending time on choosing the ideal position for them. If your winters are cold *H. serrata* does have the advantage of being more cold hardy than the typical *H. macrophylla*, surviving down to Zone 5 or 6. Where they are more delicate is in their tolerance of sun and wind. Unlike the glossy-leafed *H. macrophylla*, these dainties won't enjoy being in a windy site. The softer leaves make them more prone to sunburn and also wilting.

In the woods in Japan and Korea these plants grow naturally in deciduous forests where they are shaded from the heat of the high summer sun, so ideally we should duplicate this setting and grow them under deciduous trees such as birches and maples. There is another reason to grow them in semi-shade, especially the white-flowered varieties. The delicate pale blooms will scorch in hot sun, ruining the whole display for the remainder of the summer. In semi-shade, varieties such as 'Preziosa', 'Glyn Church' and 'Grayswood' gradually change from a rich cream to pure white then take on a light pink tinge before turning blood-red and even a rich dark red-wine color. Given heavy shade, these same blooms will turn a delectable pale green.

Hydrangea quercifolia 'Snow Queen'

Hydrangeas In and Around the House

Indoor potted plants

As we've already seen, the majority of the *Hydrangea macrophylla* types are grown as potted plants for indoor decoration, so they are quite happy in a squat container. Typically the plants are thrown away when the flowers eventually fade. There's no reason you couldn't plant them in the garden or place them in a larger pot to flower again next summer. The only drawback is many of the potted varieties have been especially selected to perform in pots and they may not necessarily be the best varieties for our garden.

My own preference is to buy potted hydrangeas for the house and discard them at the end of flowering. I know this may seem wasteful, but the plants are so cheap to begin with, it hardly matters. The way they flower endlessly for months, you're going to get value for money from them anyway. I find they are so inexpensive it's not worth the bother of repotting them for next year, and as for planting them outside later, I would rather choose a variety I know will perform well in my garden.

Tips for container growing

Some of you may want to grow these potted hydrangeas in a window box or in

OPPOSITE: Hydrangea macrophylla 'Hobella' in the antique coloring phrase makes a wonderful small container plant for indoors.

RIGHT: Grouped with other potted plants of similar shades, hydrangeas are ideal for displays in outdoor living areas.

LEFT: *Hydrangea macrophylla 'Romance'*

RIGHT: *Hydrangea macrophylla 'Harlequin'*

larger tubs for outdoor living areas. Hydrangeas are ideal for such displays and the following advice will help you achieve good results.

Buy good quality potting mix and make sure it's free draining, preferably containing plenty of coarse peat or crushed pine bark. Hydrangeas have masses of fine feeding roots near the surface and enjoy an open mix through which to send their roots in search of nutrients and moisture. Using soil from your garden is a no-no as it soon packs down like cement and the poor roots will not be able to breathe. Remember plant roots need air as well as water.

Check to see if your potting mix has added fertilizer. If not, then buy some long-term fertilizer with slow-release nutrients capable of feeding the plant over the next five to six months. My preference is to use long-term, slow-release granules. These beads of coated fertilizer slowly release the nutrients over a long period. You can buy different terms such as three-, six- or twelve-month gradual release. The expensive types release the fertilizer according to temperature, so the warmer the weather, the faster the nutrients become available, tying in nicely with the extra plant growth as the summer progresses.

Shrubs of *H. macrophylla* are hungry and thirsty plants compared with many others, so it pays to feed them properly and water regularly. Container-grown hydrangeas respond well to liquid feeding on a regular basis, but whatever the fertilizing regime, they must have plenty of water to keep healthy and perform well.

It's very easy to grow red or white varieties in a container but much more difficult to achieve good blues (see page 37). The difficulty with growing blue hydrangeas in pots is the lack of free aluminum, essential for blues, in most potting mixes. A regular dosing of aluminum sulfate will help achieve the desired colors.

Hydrangeas as cut flowers

Not only will hydrangeas decorate your home as potted color, but you can also enjoy them as cut flowers. Most flowers you buy from a florist will last for 10 to 14 days and if you're really lucky for 20 days. Hydrangea flowers will easily outlast all the competition and can stay fresh for weeks, if not months. Some say they are difficult to blend with other flowers, but why worry when they look so good on their own.

All you have to do is place a few heads in a vase and you have an instant arrangement. The smaller round heads are fine when mixed with other flowers, but the larger mops tend to dominate and look best on their own. Lacecap flowers can be a problem because they shed seeds and dust and generally make a mess.

H. paniculata and *H. quercifolia* are also wonderful cut flowers, especially near the fall when the flowers harden up and take on those delicious pink tinges.

Even quite large hydrangeas work well in containers. Here they soften the end of a house with other potted plants, large and small.

Keeping the flowers fresh and wilt-free

Hydrangea flowers have a tendency to wilt within hours of cutting. There are ways to reduce the likelihood of this happening and methods of keeping them turgid. Only cut green stems and avoid older dry brown wood as it does not take up water as easily as the younger stems. Short stocky stems are best for picking, as the longer the stems are the more likely they are to wilt because the water has further to travel.

Remove all the leaves, except possibly the top pair, as they will rob the stem of moisture. Cut ½ in. (2 cm) off the base of the stem just before arranging in your vase so the new cut will absorb moisture. If you come back an hour or so later and the heads have wilted you can immerse the whole flower and stem in a bath of cold water. They will soon pump up again with this fresh water. Ideally, leave them immersed for at least an hour, preferably two. Then make another cut at the base of the stem and rearrange the vase.

There are chemicals you can add to the water in the vase. Ask your florist for products that help keep flowers firm and make them last longer.

New soft flowers in early summer are more likely to wilt as the stems and flowers may not have firmed enough. Later in the season the problem is less likely. If you wait until the flowers have turned to antique colors in the fall they are almost guaranteed to hold firm.

Dried flowers

To many people the use of dried hydrangea flowers is a modern innovation. While it seems to have caught the imagination recently, the idea has been around for ages. Our grandmothers knew about preserving dried hydrangea flowers and part of the reason is that it is so easy to do. While a lot of flowers need fussy drying and airing to achieve good results, the heads of hydrangeas can be easily transformed into something magical by everyone.

In late summer the large sterile sepals of *H. macrophylla* flowers turn over, each one turning turtle to face inside out. Strangely enough, the flowerheads still somehow look the same after this inversion. When the sepals twist, the flowers then change color in response to cool fall nights as the sap descends in preparation for winter. Some take on a light-green hue, others a smoky-pink or metallic range, while still others deepen into rich reds and burgundies. This is the time to cut them for dried flowers. The dense heads of *H. paniculata* and *H. quercifolia* also make good dried flowers when they change to pink antique shades in the fall.

Cut all hydrangeas on a fine day when the flowers are as dry as possible, to prevent later rotting. It is possible to take longer stems for dried flowers than for fresh flowers as the water in the stems is not so crucial. Remove the leaves and put the stems in water. After a week or so the flower texture will change, becoming more rigid and paper-like. At this point you can throw away the

Drying flowerheads in antique colors. Successfully dried hydrangea blooms can last indoors through to the next flowering season.

water and the flowerheads will remain perfect throughout winter without any more moisture.

Some people recommend cutting the flowers and putting them in vases without water, or drying them in a dry, dark, warm place for a week or two before using them in arrangements. Another method is to hang the blooms upside down in a dry shed for a week or two. Explore these techniques and see which works best for you.

Once processed, you will have a posy of dried flowers capable of brightening up your room for the winter months. These heads may even last a whole year, but they do gradually fade and of course they gather dust and eventually look jaded and shabby. By that time it will be summer and your bushes in the garden will have fresh blooms again.

Good varieties for dried flowers include the *H. macrophylla* cultivars 'Altona' and 'Hamburg' in the rich blues to wine colors, and 'Générale Vicomtesse de Vibraye' and 'Maréchal Foch' in the paler blues. 'Otaksa' turns from a nondescript pale blue to a delectable shade of pale green. In the lacecaps, 'Lilacina' with its rich mix of colors, the white-turned-pink 'Veitchii' and also *H. serrata* 'Grayswood' are all good subjects.

Species and Cultivars

Hydrangea arborescens

H. arborescens is one of the two North American species. It has the distinction of being the first hydrangea to be introduced into cultivation in the West. The name "arborescens" means "treelike," and in the wild it can grow to 10 ft. (3 m), but it is usually between 3 and 6 ft. (1–1.8 m) high in a garden. (Many of the Chinese species are distinctly more treelike than *H. arborescens*.)

In the wild this wide-ranging species is found from New York State all through the Appalachian Mountains down to Florida, growing in shady, moist sites. It can be a little difficult to please in warm, moist climates unless attention is paid to good drainage to prevent root rot. It seems to tolerate moist sites in a cooler climate. All forms of *H. arborescens* will endure severe cold, tolerating harsh winters down to Zone 3, and garden varieties of this species are well worth growing as excellent replacements for mophead hydrangeas in colder climates.

H. arborescens plants are also very drought-resistant. Some forms are likely to sucker, sending up new plants from underground. This is rarely a problem in a garden situation and easily controlled and may be put to good use to propagate new plants. The leaves are typically hairy and thin, in a neat heart shape and usually pale green. The leaves turn a pleasant butter yellow in the fall.

OPPOSITE: *Hydrangea arborescens* 'Annabelle' in a mass display.

RIGHT: The flowerhead of *H. arborescens* 'Annabelle'.

The wild form has a small lacecap flower in subdued white. There are two subspecies. All forms are equally happy in sun or shade and are rarely attacked by pests and diseases. While the wild forms have a lacecap flower, there have been some selections made of sterile flower forms, with flowers ranging from the size of a fist to huge ball-like flowers all in creamy-white. The blooms are so big the stems are often bowed over by their weight.

H. arborescens subsp. *radiata* has more garden merit than straight *H. arborescens*, forming a large, upright, tidy shrub. The sweetly scented large white lacecaps, held above the bush, are attractively displayed. The splendid heart-shaped leaves are slightly hairy above and covered in velvety silver hairs on the reverse. This is a charming woodland plant for larger gardens. Found naturally at higher elevations, it is not as heat tolerant as other forms of *H. arborescens*. It grows to 10 ft. (3 m).

H. arborescens subsp. *discolor* is another wild form with a white lacecap flower and slightly hairy leaves that are dull green on the reverse. It grows to 10 ft. (3 m).

H. arborescens subsp. *radiata*—note the bright silver of the reversed leaf.

Good garden varieties for cooler areas

'**Annabelle**' is a marvelous form. Very large heads of white sterile flowers make this an outstanding shrub for any garden. The flowerheads can be so heavy it is impossible for the shrub to keep them upright. Some people recommend severe pruning every winter to encourage strong new growth capable of supporting the huge blooms. Eventually, as the plant gets bigger it gets stronger and more able to hold the heads upright. 'Annabelle' needs a sheltered site away from wind because of these large blooms. In late summer the heads turn green and are very good for using as cut or dried flowers. This hydrangea is much more showy than the species, but it lacks the grace of the wild plant. Gardeners in regions of lower temperatures are especially appreciative of its ability to produce flowers on new stems even when the cold cuts the plant to ground level. It usually grows around 5–6 ft. (1.5–1.8 m), but it can grow much larger.

'**Grandiflora**' has slightly uneven, almost pointed, mopheads of pure white sterile flowers. This plant looks truly beautiful when established, though it does have an untidy weeping habit in the early years. The flowerheads can be so heavy the plant droops with the weight. The plant grows to 5 ft. (1.5 m) and the blooms make excellent cut flowers.

'**Hayes Starburst**' Appropriately named, as the multi-sepaled flowers look just like a starburst, this was discovered as a seedling in Hayes Jackson's Alabama garden. It has a low, tidy habit and would be an ideal choice for gardeners with limited space, as it grows to 6 ft. (1.8 m).

'**Mary Nell**' The flower is a unique sort of lacecap with groups of sterile flowers clustered around and through the true flowers, giving the impression of a lacecap on steroids. The plant is named after the wife of the late Joe McDaniel, who was head of Horticulture at the University of Illinois. Among other things he discovered *H. a.* 'Annabelle'. 'Mary Nell' grows to 6 ft. (1.8 m).

'**Samantha**' is the perfect plant for gardeners who cannot grow the more tender macrophylla types, but want a pure white mophead hydrangea. It's a form of *H. a.* subsp. *radiata* and so has the fascinating silver reverse leaves but offers the added attraction of white snowball flowers because the florets are all sterile. The plant is hardy, compact (5 ft., 1.5 m) and beautiful, but does not thrive in hot climates.

'**White Dome**' is perfectly named as the flower is a neat dome of white lace. Because the flowers are light, the bush keeps a good shape and doesn't collapse. Leaves are silvery-white beneath, showing *H. a. radiata* blood. The plant is often reluctant to flower and the flowers can be small. Also known as 'Dardom', it grows to 7 ft. (2 m).

A few pink forms of *H. arborescens* have recently come onto the market. They are strongly pink or even purple at the bud stage and then open to white. Look out for '**Chestatee**', '**Eco Pink Puff**', '**Pink Pincushion**' and '**Wesser Falls**'.

TOP: H. arborescens 'Hayes Starburst'
ABOVE: H. arborescens 'White Dome'

H. aspera

H. aspera is a variable and widespread species mostly found in western China and through the Himalayas. This species now includes lots of popular garden hydrangeas previously known under names like *H. sargentiana* and *H. villosa*. These are now all classified as subspecies of *H. aspera*, though just to confuse the issue, recent DNA evidence suggests *H. villosa* is a species in its own right. Typically, *H. aspera* plants have hairy, bristly leaves that make a noise when you rub them between your fingers. The lacecap flowers usually have pink or white sterile sepals surrounding purple-blue true flowers. The contrast between pink and purple can be quite stunning. Gardeners should seek out the named forms as they are truly beautiful.

Robust and easy to grow, eventually reaching 10 ft. (3 m) or more, these shrubs are really only suitable for large woodland gardens. Not fussy about soils and happy in full sun or semi-shade, they are usually frost-hardy to Zone 6 or 7. A mild, moist climate seems to suit them best. Hot, dry climates cause them to suffer even though they are drought tolerant. Having virtually no pest or disease problems is a bonus.

H. a. subsp. *sargentiana* was once considered a species in its own right. It was named after Charles Sargent of Arnold Arboretum fame. Sargent went plant-hunting in Japan and later helped classify the plants of Ernest Wilson, who collected this plant in China. It is considered one of the choicest hydrangeas, sought after by many gardening enthusiasts. Having said that, it is rather rare and can be difficult to cultivate. It is also tricky to propagate, which adds to the scarcity value. As well as being difficult to grow from cuttings, it produces very few stems, unlike most hydrangeas. In winter the few thick bare stems it produces look rather like deer antlers, with thick bristly hairs all along the branches.

The large lacecap flowers have pink-hued white sterile flowers surrounding smoky-mauve to lilac true flowers. The main appeal, however, lies in the huge bristly leaves that make it one of the top foliage plants. Growing to 10 ft. (3 m), *H. a.* subsp. *sargentiana* forms a very big suckering shrub that is suitable for large gardens and parks.

H. a. subsp. *villosa*, a favorite of mine, bears pink and mauve lacecap flowers throughout late summer. Another shrub collected in Western China by Ernest Wilson, this hydrangea tolerates alkaline soil, is reasonably drought resistant, and is more likely to die of poor drainage than frost. Cold hardy, growing to Zone 7, it has leaves and stems that are densely villous and this hairy foliage protects it against wind and cold. Of fairly dense structure and very full looking, it grows up to 10 ft. (3 m) in full sun or just a morsel of shade. Because of the narrow pointed leaves it blends well with rhododendrons and looks good at the back of a border, ideally with a dark backdrop of evergreen shrubs to show off the flowers. Considered too big for town gardens, it definitely earns a place in any large woodland planting. Combined with a drift of pink *Anemone hupehensis,* it will set your late summer garden on fire.

Some of the *H. aspera* cultivars worth searching for

'**Mauvette**' is a delightful form with mauve true and sterile flowers in a dome-shaped lacecap. These large flowerheads are 6 in. (15 cm) across and are at their best around midsummer. The sterile florets gradually fade to a pinky-gray while the fertile flowers tend to go red. This makes an excellent dried flower and grows to 10 ft. (3 m). The bush needs a sheltered site.

'**Peter Chappell**' is a lovely form selected by Maurice Foster and worthy of greater popularity. It has large furry leaves and stems and grows to 7 ft. (2 m). The beautiful informal lacecaps have white sterile florets surrounding creamy-pink true flowers.

'**Pink Cloud**' was discovered in western China by Roy Lancaster. It has beautiful large hairy leaves topped with very soft pink flowers.

H. macrophylla

H. macrophylla is the type most people envisage when hydrangeas are mentioned. This species is undoubtedly the most popular and well known of all the hydrangeas. The name "macrophylla" means "big leaf," referring to the very large bold leaves of this species. *H. macrophylla* comes originally from Japan and has caused botanists much confusion. Some believe it is a naturally occurring species while others maintain it is of hybrid origin. The plants in cultivation under the name of *H. macrophylla* 'Seafoam' and the one that J.P. Commerson introduced as *H. opuloides* germinate freely in my garden and though there is some variation, it's no more than one sees in other plant species.

In nature this species has a lacecap flower, with white to the palest flax-blue sterile florets and true flowers of dark sea-blue. The mophead types were just a naturally occurring "sport." Breeders have taken these round-headed sports and bred from them to produce more colorful mopheads. Hydrangeas 'Ayesha', 'Otaksa' and 'Sir Joseph Banks' are probably sports of the wild *H. macrophylla.*

The natural species have very glossy leaves and this allows them to cope with salt winds. Of the many cultivars, some have inherited this ability to cope with coastal conditions. For the most part they are resilient plants, tolerating shade, sun, wet soil, and virtually anything the elements and gardeners can throw at them, including frost, though this may cause growth to weaken, or lose flowers for the coming summer. They are quite hardy, growing from Zones 6 and 7 through to Zone 10.

Before I discuss actual cultivars, it's worth reflecting on the two types of

Hydrangea macrophylla '*Otaksa*'

Hydrangea macrophylla
'Immaculata'

H. macrophylla flowers. The familiar mopheads are the best value as the flowers are nearly all sterile and cannot be pollinated. This means the flowers go on and on all through summer until the cooler nights of fall, when they take on another color. Growers term this stage of the flower's life "antique" because the petals have an "olde worlde" look. Some of the color changes are dramatic: brilliant blues can turn to wine-red, and whites can change to pale green and even brilliant blood-red.

Lacecap flowers, those flat macrophylla heads with true flowers in the center surrounded by a ring of sterile petals, are the other kind. When they're fresh, these flowers are superb and there's often a contrasting color between the true and sterile florets, but because the true flowers will be pollinated by insects the lacecaps will fade much faster than the mophead types. When the flowers have been pollinated the sterile florets will turn turtle and then change color with the action of sunlight, becoming antique like the mopheads. Typically, a lacecap flower will look good for a month compared to three, four or even six months for the mopheads.

H. macrophylla cultivars

'**Adria**' A stunning sea blue as you might expect from a plant named after the Adriatic Sea. It's perfect for pots and tubs, being a small compact plant and ideal for border edging. It needs acid soil to be the perfect blue and is not suitable for alkaline soils. Grows to 3 ft. (1 m).

'**Agnes Pavelli**' One of the best white mophead hydrangeas, forming a moderate-sized, tidy bush covered in neat domes of pure white flowers with clean, smooth-edged sepals. 'Agnes Pavelli' is reasonably tolerant of full sun and does not scorch as quickly as most other whites. In fact, the fall colors of the flower are often a scintillating burgundy. This variety has very serrated leaves, and is a good foil for some of the richer colored hydrangeas. It grows to 5 ft. (1.5 m).

'**All Summer Beauty**' An excellent shrub for cold regions, being hardy and robust. It's also one of the newer remontant cultivars capable of sending up new flower shoots if the plant is frosted in spring. Neat mophead flower in pink or pale blue. Very similar to "Nikko Blue" and "Générale Vicomtesse de Vibraye" but has glossy leaves. Grows to around 5 ft. (1.5 m).

'**Alpenglühen**' (syn. '**Alpenglow**' and '**Glowing Embers**') A lovely rosy-red mophead, even in slightly acid soil. It has nicely shaped rounded heads and makes a perfect cut flower bloom. This is an easy-care, robust variety growing to 5 ft. (1.5 m).

BELOW LEFT: Hydrangea macrophylla 'Adria'

BELOW: Hydrangea macrophylla 'Agnes Pavelli'

BOTTOM: Hydrangea macrophylla 'Alpenglühen'

FROM TOP: Hydrangea macrophylla 'Altona'

Hydrangea macrophylla 'Amethyst'

Hydrangea macrophylla 'Arthur Billard'

Hydrangea macrophylla 'Beauté Vendômoise'

'Altona' This plant should suit nearly everyone as it's a good pink in lime and an excellent French blue in acid soils. In soils that are neither strongly acid nor alkaline, 'Altona' still has a charming combination of pinky-mauve with white centers, with the more open older flowers tending to blue. Many varieties need to be strongly red or strongly blue to look their best, but 'Altona' always looks good. It's very floriferous and is typically smothered in bloom. 'Altona' is happy in sun or shade and is one of the best varieties for windy or coastal gardens, but is prone to frost damage inland. It grows to 7 ft. (2 m). A very good cut flower and as a bonus the flowers turn to delicious antique colors in the fall. Popular as an indoor pot plant because it shines whatever the flower color.

'Amethyst' A compact little plant growing just over 3 ft. (1 m) with round ruffled blooms. The flowers vary from pale violet-blue to soft pink depending on the acidity. It's perfect for small gardens and narrow borders under windows where you can appreciate the semi-double flowers at close range. Being close to the house will give added protection as it's prone to frost damage.

'Ami Pasquier' A charming bush with small round heads of rich crimson to Tyrian purple. One of the best crimson reds for alkaline soils and a pretty maroon in acid soil. This compact plant with good foliage has the added appeal of its leaves turning red in the fall, which is very unusual as most macrophyllas have no fall color. Another attribute is that 'Ami Pasquier' produces new flowers all summer in remontant fashion. It grows to 5 ft. (1.5 m).

'Arthur Billard' Thought to be lost to cultivation until recently rediscovered. Once very popular for forcing, to create an early-flowering red mophead. The color is very intense and the flowers remain a modest size, making it ideal for pot culture. One of the very few *H. macrophylla* shrubs to have fall color as the leaves turn to reds and yellows. Grows to 4 ft. (1.2 m).

'Athens' One of the new "City-Line" series. A good pink mophead and ideal for pot culture. Grows to around 3 ft. (1 m).

'Ayesha' (syn. 'Silver Slipper') A totally unique hydrangea, one that everyone can recognize at a glance because the sepals are thick and fleshy and held in a cup shape. The flower head is round like a mophead, but much smaller than most. In a neutral or limey soil the color is a beautiful soft shell-pink. In acid soils the flowers are very gentle mauve-lilac to blue. The leaves too are very distinct, being glossy and bold, and this means the plant can handle maximum sunlight and coastal gales. The plant must be a sport from another hydrangea because occasionally a branch will revert to a typical macrophylla flower in soft shell-pink. It grows to 7 ft. (2 m).

'Beauté Vendômoise' Although this variety was bred way back in 1909 by Emile Mouillère it is still a phenomenal plant. The flowers are huge lacecaps—the size of a dinner plate—surrounded by enormous sterile florets up to 5 in. (12 cm) wide. Despite the huge size of the blooms, the plant has loads of

Hydrangea macrophylla 'Blaumeise'

charm. The sterile florets are the palest butterfly-blue in acid soil and the softest pink in alkaline ground. These sometimes emerge through the true flowers, which some say spoils the flat lacecap effect. The flowers are scented, which is a bonus. The large strong bush (height 10 ft. or 3 m) would look out of place in a small suburban garden, but offers much potential for larger, informal and park-like landscapes.

'Blaumeise' (syns. 'Blue Meise', 'Blue Tit', 'Blue Sky', 'Teller Blue') One of the Swiss-bred Teller hybrids. The name when translated means "blue tit," a small European bird. "Teller" is a German word for "plate," referring to the flat lacecap flowers. Most of the Teller hybrids are named after European birds

Hydrangea macrophylla
'Blue Wave'

and sometimes appear under their English translation names.

'Blaumeise' has beautiful cobalt blue florets surrounding the fertile Persian blue true flowers in genuine lacecap fashion. It can be a pleasing soft pink in limey soils. The heads are quite small and have a tidy, almost pristine appearance. Grow them in a dell where you can admire the flowers from above. It grows to 7 ft. (2 m).

'Blue Prince' ('Blauer Prinz') In an acid soil it's a simply stupendous cobalt blue with very small round heads. The bush is small too, growing around 3 ft. (1 m) high, and so the mophead flowers are in proportion to the plant. Don't grow this variety in alkaline soils as the flower color is a wishy-washy pink.

'Blue Wave' The perfect plant for coastal gardens and for planting in large groups or as a hedge. The masses of true blue lacecaps are stunning en masse. The foliage is good too, being glossy and a rich dark green. Unfortunately the flowers are a muddy color in lime soils and for these gardens 'Blaumeise' is an easier blue. This is a tall hardy plant, growing 5–7 ft. (or 1.5–2 m) and is happy in sun or shade.

'Bodensee' A very popular pink mophead well suited to growing in pots and tubs as it has a second flush of flowers late in the summer. Becomes a passable

Hydrangea macrophylla 'Bodensee'

blue in acid soil and the flowers have a smooth outer appearance as if groomed. It is a dense, compact plant with pale but attractive foliage that grows to 4 ft. (1.2 m). Its dwarf habit, long flowering season and healthy nature make it an ideal garden shrub. Sometimes used for the cut flower trade.

'**Bouquet Rose**' This is one of the oldest hybrid hydrangeas available. Although it has been superseded by stronger colors, it still has a certain charm. In alkaline soils the mopheads are soft pink; they become a very pale pinky-violet in acid soil. In fall the flowers change into hues of green and violet, creating excellent dried subjects. Also, as these flowers tend to change color long before most other varieties, they can be picked early in the season for drying. The rather weak stems tend to bow with the weight of the mopheads, but this somehow adds to the allure of the plant. It is a very frost-hardy bush that grows to 7 ft. (2 m). It is not everyone's first choice, but a valuable garden plant nonetheless.

'**Bridal Bouquet**' A fairly new white cultivar that grows to only 3 ft. (1 m) high, this is ideal for pots and tubs because of its dwarf habit. Has neat, clean-edged, cup-shaped cream to white flowers and is happy in sun or shade as long as the soil is not too dry. It is very similar to 'Immaculata', which is the best of the dwarf white mopheads.

'City-Line' series Bred and introduced by the Rampp Nursery in Germany, these mopheads are excellent cultivars but, annoyingly, one has been named 'Hamburg' and another 'Paris' despite there being cultivars with these names already. This is totally against the rules of plant naming and only serves to confuse. See also 'Athens' and 'Venice'.

'Claudie' Introduced by Corinne Mallet of the famed Shamrock hydrangea collection in Varengeville sur Mer, near Dieppe, France. This hydrangea is named after and dedicated to Claudie André-Deshays, a French astronaut. It is a delightful lacecap with starry pinky-mauve to blue flowers that can be likened to the stars orbiting the heavens. Grows to 5 ft. (1.5 m).

'Colonel Durham' Surely one of the best pink mopheads—clean round balls in a clear vibrant color. Is quite a pleasing mauve in acid soils. Good distinctive foliage is a bonus. 5 ft. (1.5 m).

'Domotoi' This delightful mophead hydrangea is quite unusual because the flowers are double. The overlapping sepals have a porcelain appearance, highlighted by the frilly edges. In acid soil the flowers are an enchanting pale butterfly-blue. In alkaline soils it's a soft baby pink and it does make lovely cut flowers for the house.

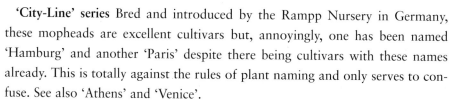

Ideal for small gardens as it grows to not much more than 3 ft. (1 m) high. The foliage is sometimes spotty and pale, but the mass of flowers disguises these faults.

'**Dooley**' Selected by Michael Dirr for being a valuable remontant capable of flowering in colder regions and because it is so floriferous. The large round heads are pink or blue, depending on your soil. A vigorous healthy plant suitable for most regions. Grows to 6 ft. (1.8 m).

'**Emotion**' A fabulous new double hydrangea from Japan. Part of a series bred by Ryoji Irie, a plant breeder and rock guitarist in Kyoto. The series are collectively known as the 'YOU-ME' series. 'Emotion' has huge double pink flowers in a lacecap shape except that the inner flowers are double as well. The flowers in the outer circle open first, followed gradually by the inner flowers, which create a frothy haze of pink petals. Ideal in pots and tubs. Grows to 3 ft. (1 m).

ABOVE: **Hydrangea macrophylla 'Emotion'**

BELOW: **Hydrangea macrophylla 'Dooley'**

TOP: *Hydrangea macrophylla* 'Enziandom'
ABOVE: *Hydrangea macrophylla* 'Endless Summer'

'**Endless Summer**' Perfectly named as it is remontant and therefore capable of producing new flowers all summer. Ideal for cold regions as the bush can still manage to produce flowers despite spring frosts killing canes that carry overwintering buds. This mophead is becoming justifiably famous in the colder regions of North America where previously it was impossible to have blooming hydrangeas. For inland gardeners who have never grown hydrangeas before, this would be a treat. Neat rounded mopheads in pink or pale violet-blue. Grows 3–5 ft. (1–1.5 m).

'**Enziandom**' (syn. '**Gentian Dome**') A big bold plant with lush rich green foliage that looks good enough to eat. The heads of blue are solid and rather weighty, but held aloft on stout stems. The color in an acid soil is the most scintillating gentian-blue. The heads have a nice clean appearance with the dense domes up to 10 in. (25 cm) across made up of large, smooth-edged sepals. Terrific cut flowers in summer, they turn a metallic blue in the antique phase. 5 ft. (1.5 m).

'Eternity' Another in the 'YOU-ME' series from Ryoji Irie in Kyoto, Japan. Like 'Emotion', these flat-topped blooms have large double flowers opening from the outside toward the center. The flowers are smooth and edged in a rich pink with a delightful creamy center. 3 ft. (1 m).

'Europa' An old variety that tends to grow very tall, but produces a very agreeable pink mophead or a passable mauve-blue in acid soils. Up close, the frilly-edged sepals and cup shape of each floret add to the appeal, particularly for cut flowers. Creates a very good dried flower too. It does tend to be a muddy color in neutral soils and there are better varieties available. However, because of its vigor, it makes an excellent hedge or backdrop for a border. 7 ft. (2 m).

'Fasan' (syn. 'Pheasant', 'Twilight') "Fasan" is German for "pheasant," a bird with a bright red wattle on its head, and the heads on this Teller lacecap can be a similar stunning red when grown in alkaline soil. The large sterile flowers are distinctly pointed and tend to be in a double row, almost masking the true flowers at times. This hydrangea is sensitive to late frost, which can reduce the number of flowers. It forms a bold upright plant to 5 ft. (1.5 m). In acid or neutral soils the flowers are a rather dull violet color.

'Forever' has lovely double flowers on a flattish-topped head that's halfway between a mophead and a lacecap. The color is a delicious shade of soft shell pink, which if grown in shade will antique to pleasing shades of green. In an acid soil the flowers become a smoky blue. Growing to 3 ft. (1 m) this is another in the 'YOU-ME' series from Ryoji Irie in Kyoto, Japan.

'Frau Fujiyo', 'Frau Taiko', 'Frau Katsuko'—see **Japanese Lady** series.

'Freudenstein' Creating large heads of excellent pink to Persian rose in alkaline soil, the flowers of this cultivar become blue with a hint of purple in acid mix. They have very large florets with gaps between the sepals. The low dense bush (around 3 ft. or 1 m) is ideal for tubs except that it's prone to mildew when stressed.

BELOW FROM LEFT:
Hydrangea macrophylla 'Eternity'

Hydrangea macrophylla 'Forever'

Hydrangea macrophylla 'Freudenstein'

TOP: *Hydrangea macrophylla* 'Frillibet'

ABOVE: *Hydrangea macrophylla* 'Geoffrey Chadbund'

'**Frillibet**' I love the color, but sometimes despair about the plant. The frilly-edged sepals in the softest powder blue or pale pink are simply delicious, but the plant has pale leaves and a rather weak constitution and structure. After a few years the bush eventually holds the heads up properly and seems to perform quite well. Unlike most *H. macrophylla* varieties it seems to need coddling for the first few years. Best in partial shade as the flowers burn in strong sunlight, it grows to 4 ft. (1.2 m). 'Frillibet' was selected and named by Michael Haworth-Booth, who in the 1950s wrote the first and most comprehensive book on hydrangeas.

'**Gartenbaudirektor Kühnert**' It is becoming a firm favorite of mine because it performs so well every summer. The dense mopheads open straight to sky blue, a true mid-blue, and they look terrific for months. The plant is often a little late flowering, but more than compensates by continuing to flower when the blooms of most other varieties have turned to brown. The sterile florets are clean, smooth-edged and without frills and it's a lovely cut flower. Not recommended for alkaline soils as the flower color will be muddy. It grows to 5 ft. (1.5 m).

'**General Patton**' A compact dense bush that grows to just over 3 ft. (1 m) high, this has pleasant rosy-red flowers in tight heads. It tends to keep a reddish color even in slightly acid soils, but can change to violet in very acid ground. This is an easy to grow, healthy variety with superb foliage of rich dark green and perfect leaf patterns. It's underrated and would make a superb potted plant as it has the best foliage of all the cultivars.

'**Générale Vicomtesse de Vibraye**' Simply beautiful hydrangea with the palest sky-blue mopheads. The small flowerheads open soft cream, almost yellow before taking on the blue tinges. The flowers have a smooth, clean, almost manicured look. In the fall the flowers turn green, thus making it a very special dried flower for winter decoration. It makes a useful cut flower in summer too because the heads are not too bulky and easily blend with other blooms. Stems are flecked with wine-red streaks, like a bird's egg. Flowers can burn in the sun so it needs plenty of moisture or a little shade. This variety is also notable for its reflexed leaves with a tropical drip-end. Tropical plants have a long thin tip to the leaves to shed water much faster than ordinary leaves, which presumably helps them cope with tropical downpours. These leaves are pale in color but in no way detract from the plant. In fact the light-colored foliage sets off the pale blue flowers much better than very dark leaves would. This hydrangea produces lots of flowers per bush and should it lose its terminal flowers to frost, it happily produces more blooms from below in remontant fashion. It grows to 5 ft. (1.5 m).

'**Geoffrey Chadbund**' This outstanding lacecap deserves to be more well known. The large sterile flowers are spiraea-red, turning to rose or magenta in alkaline or slightly acid soils. The flowerhead has the perfect lacecap shape with a neat flat top and perfect rounded sepals and appeals to tidy gardeners. It grows to 5 ft. (1.5 m).

'**Green Shadow**' You may wonder how a red hydrangea came to have the name "green." In fact this delightful red mophead has quite dark green tinges instead of the usual yellow when the flower is opening, before turning true red. Almost immediately afterwards, it again seems to take on a green hue, making it interesting and different. It is becoming popular as a cut flower and potted plant. Grows to 4 ft. (1.2 m).

'**Hamburg**' A stupendous plant with enormous mopheads. The flowerhead has huge sterile florets, some serrated, some simple and some kidney-shaped, yet for all this it presents as a clean bold head of color. In acid soils it's a superb blue, not royal, not rich, not sky, just plain and simple blue. It maintains this color all through summer, changing to the most incredible wine-red in fall when it is simply stunning as a cut flower. It has good bold dark green leaves and grows to 5 ft. (1.5 m). To increase the size of the heads, prune to reduce the

Hydrangea macrophylla '*Générale Vicomtesse de Vibraye*'

overall number of flowers so the strength is put into a few super-duper blooms. To confuse the issue there is a new 'City Line' hydrangea called 'Hamburg' with pink mopheads. Make sure you buy the good one—the original one!

'**Hanabi**' Shiny leaves give the clue this plant can handle salt winds. The white lacecap flowers are starry doubles and the shrub has some appeal as an indoor potted plant. Sometimes sold as 'Fireworks'. Grows to 7 ft. (2 m).

'**Harlequin**' This unusual hydrangea was known as '**Sensation**' for many years. It has a rounded head of red flowers and each sepal has a frilly white edge or outline, making it a lively two-toned or variegated flower. It's not to everyone's taste, as it does not blend easily with other shrubs, but it probably has a place as a tub plant near the house. Best sited on a terrace or patio as it is rather frost tender. It grows to 4 ft. (1.2 m). Can be a very weak plant with a poor constitution.

'**Harry's Red**' has fabulous round heads of pure crimson. These are borne on a small to medium bush (3 ft. or 1 m), not the most robust of shrubs but it earns its place as one of the best reds available. Even in acid soils it tends to stay close to red. It has good, rich flower colors in fall and is ideal for small gardens. Strangely enough, this is not a well-known variety and deserves far greater popularity as it is one of the best compact reds.

'**Heinrich Seidel**' (syn. '**Glory of Aalsmeer**') I used to be scathing about this variety with its nondescript neither red nor blue flowers. Now it's a firm favorite. It has frilly-edged sepals on good-sized mopheads in light red in lime soil or a delicious lilac in acid soil. Seems to handle sun, wind and shade and is a fabulous antique. It forms a tall upright plant to 7 ft. (2 m).

'Hobella' This is a recent Dutch-bred plant with delightful soft pink flowers. Technically a lacecap, though the center is often full of sterile flowers creating a flat-top lacecap. Initially it's a delicious shell pink, then the flowers change color, the outer sepals turning green and then red in the antique phase, when it makes a superb cut flower. The flowers tend to scorch if grown in too much sunlight, so choose a shady spot for this shrub that grows to 4 ft. (1.2 m). Sometimes used as a potted plant. Bred by Koos and Wilko Hofstede.

'Homigo' Another new Dutch mophead from Hovaria. It's a neat compact plant, but the flower colors are the highlight. Starts as a pleasing light blue in early summer, changing to red in the antique stage. Grows to 5 ft. (1.5 m).

'Hopaline' Third in the Dutch series from Hovaria, this small mophead plant begins blooming as a pale soft pink before turning green and then to red in the antique phase. A fascinating potted plant. Grows to 4 ft. (1.2 m).

'Hopcorn' is a brand-new novelty, a sport from 'Mathilda Gutges' discovered by Koos and Wilko Hofstede in Holland. The petals are cupped and fleshy, somewhat like 'Ayesha' but in a much richer purple-maroon color. Grows to 4 ft. (1.2 m).

'Hörnli' A superb dwarf, just ideal for patio pots and tubs. For me it's the best true dwarf hydrangea by a long way and a lot better than 'Piamina'. Cute pinky-red smooth mopheads decorate the small (8–12 in., 20–30 cm) rounded plant. Sometimes sold as **'Success'**. Can be a bit temperamental when young.

'Immaculata' A low-growing, dense bush with rich green foliage. The flowers open a delicious shade of cream, changing to pure white. Ideally this hydrangea needs to be grown in shade to prevent burning or sun scorch. If you can prevent the flowers from burning in the hot summer sun it will reward you with an antique shade, turning bright red with sunlight and green in shade. It also makes a terrific container plant in a shady location. Usually grows around 3 ft. (1 m).

'Izu-no-Hana' This plant is still growing on me. Initially I dismissed it for having a weak constitution and haphazard flowering but now, after a few years, the bushes have built up strength and I'm more excited about the plant and its intriguing blooms. The lacecap flowers are double with all sorts of interesting twirls in soft pink to purple, depending on the soil acidity. The foliage is very dark and shiny, but often the leaves are narrow and sometimes distorted. It grows to 5 ft. (1.5 m). 'Izu-no-Hana' translates as "Flower of the Izu Peninsula," which is the region where the wild *H. macrophylla* is found.

'Japanese Lady' series ('Frau Fujiyo', 'Frau Taiko', 'Frau Katsuko') Simply gorgeous to look at but beset by problems, these shrubs with fabulous two-tone mophead flowers have an unfortunate weak constitution and often fade away or simply die. As the saying goes: "When they're good, they're very good, but when they're not they're ...." ('Harlequin' has similar coloring and similar problems.) Typically if you plant five of these, two will die, two will look stunted and miserable and the other one will be fabulous. Everyone sees the fabulous specimen and wants to buy one for themselves!

'Jogasaki' A relatively new introduction from Japan with double lacecap flowers. These have a very good shape and fully double sterile florets in silver pink. Becomes a good blue in acid soil. Forms a big, strong, wind-hardy plant (to 7 ft. or 2 m) but has one major drawback, being prone to black spot disease.

'Kardinal' A scintillating red lacecap with almost a double row of sterile flowers around the outer edge. Appropriately named, as the flowers are indeed a cardinal red. Grows to 6 ft. (1.8 m).

'Kluis Superba' An old-fashioned variety but it still has charm. Grows very tall and can be used as an informal hedge. Has deep pink or violet-blue flowers, depending on the soil, but the colors tend to fade quite quickly into antique shades. Grows to 8 ft. (2.5 m).

'Lady in Red' is a new cultivar from Michael Dirr. A very unusual lacecap hydrangea that changes from white to red, and even more remarkably has red stems and red fall foliage. High mildew resistance is a bonus. Grows to 5 ft. (1.5 m).

'La France' This is a perfect shrub for coastal gardens because it can handle salt winds. Being frost tender it needs a maritime climate. The massive round heads are soft pink to light blue. Forms a tall plant to 7 ft. (2 m) and can be used as a hedge.

Hydrangea macrophylla
'Jogasaki'

Hydrangea macrophylla
'Lanarth White'

Hydrangea macrophylla
'Leuchtfeuer'

'**La Marne**' Somewhat similar to 'La France', this medium-sized bush has large healthy leaves and huge mopheads of soft pink or blue. These large flowers have very serrated sepals. This tough, vigorous plant is ideal for coastal gardens, but is also happy inland. It has excellent fall flower colors in smoky pinks, greens and mauves. Height 5 ft. (1.5 m).

'**Lanarth White**' A pure white lacecap with mauve-pink true flowers. Sometimes the sepals are in two rows and the flower almost seems to be a mophead. It has very distinct pale green leaves with sharp points. It's a tremendous plant for tough places, coping with dry sunny sites near the coast. Height 7 ft. (2 m).

'**Le Cygne**' This old-fashioned variety is also known as '**White Swan**', a name you may find it under in garden centers, "cygne" being the French name for a cygnet or baby swan. It's a big, tough, healthy plant with small white mopheads made up of delightful frilly pointed sepals. Sometimes the heads take on a tinge of pink. 7 ft. (2 m).

'**Leuchtfeuer**' (syn. '**Lightfire**' and '**Firelight**') A strong robust pink to red with huge mophead flowers. In acid soils these bloom a dull mauve. Often used for forcing and for cut flowers. Grows to 5 ft. (1.5 m).

'**Libelle**' (syns. '**Dragonfly**', '**Snow**', '**Teller White**') Perhaps the best white lacecap. The smooth-edged sepals of pure white look so pristine surrounding the true blue flowers in the center. The contrast is stunning. Late on in high summer to fall the white sepals turn turtle and change to a subtle pink, but as the plant keeps producing new flowers the bush can have two contrasting flowers. The plant has distinctive pale-green pointy leaves and often the bush has a slightly wayward habit but it looks fine in an informal garden, especially near water. 5 ft. (1.5 m).

'Lilacina' Here's a delightful lacecap with the outer sepals in phlox pink in alkaline soil through to imperial purple in acid conditions. Internal true flowers are violet and blue. The contrast between the pinky-purple and the blue is striking. A tough, sun-tolerant bush, but the plant looks equally striking in a shady dell. Grows 5–7 ft. (1.5–2 m).

'Love You Kiss' is a stunning new cultivar with white flowers etched in red. These crinkle-cut red-edged flowers, which look good enough to eat, later fade to green and finally turn red. Bred by Mototeru Yatabe in Japan using H. 'Kiyosumi', this cultivar is also notable for its reddish leaf in the spring foliage and again in the fall.

'Luvumama' is a new remontant selected by (the late) Penny McHenry and introduced by Mal Condon. It has neat rounded pink mopheads, or rich blue in acid soils, and these are mass produced all summer. Ideal for gardeners in cooler regions because it's remontant, but also very happy in hot sunny climes. Forms a big robust healthy plant, growing to 7 ft. (2 m). Penny came up with the name 'Luvumama' because that's how her eldest daughter always signed off her telephone conversations.

'Maculata' The variegated hydrangeas are easily confused. This one has three colors, green in the center, streaks of gray and a bold white edge. It is probably the prettiest of the variegated types as 'Tricolor' looks gray from a distance and 'Quadricolor' looks rather odd with splashes of yellow. The lacecap flowers

BELOW LEFT: Hydrangea macrophylla 'Lilacina' on the left.

BELOW: Hydrangea macrophylla 'Libelle'

BOTTOM: Hydrangea macrophylla 'Love You Kiss'

are easily overlooked, but can look beautiful in a shady dell. They consist of white to pale pastel-mauve sterile florets surrounding rose-purple to violet true flowers. If you like these variegated hydrangeas you will need to site them very carefully as they are fragile, being prone to damage from cold, frost and fierce winds. Protect them from slugs and snails too as they travel great distances to feed on these varieties. It grows to 5 ft. (1.5 m).

'**Madame Baardse**' A neat little plant with intense red mops in alkaline soils. In acid soils, the flowers are a lovely soft violet. The foliage is good, being shiny and dense, and the plant is so compact it's perfect for outdoor pots and tubs. Every year this variety impresses me more and more. 3 ft. (1 m).

'**Madame Emile Mouillère**' A heavenly white mophead and just perfect for a shady dell, but equally happy in a large tub in sunshine. The reason it looks fine in both situations is the lax arching habit of the bush and because the flower heads do not get too big. Tidy gardeners may not like it. The flowers open as a creamy white but soon take on a perfect pure white. The flower heads are made up of very reflexed sepals, forming a dense, almost complete dome. Late in the fall the flowers will take on a hint of pink. Make sure the plant gets plenty of water to prevent the flowers from burning.

Ideal in coastal regions because of its glossy leaves, and yet more cold hardy than most cultivars, it makes a good beginner's plant as it is easy to grow. Often grown as an indoor plant. 6 ft. (1.8 m).

'**Madame F. Travouillon**' has very soft powder-blue mopheads. The leaves too are pale and the plant does best in shade away from the hot sun. The flowers tend to turn a pale green in the antique phase. Often used as an indoor plant because it readily blues. 5 ft. (1.5 m).

'**Madame Henri Cayeux**' Beautiful large balls of crimson red fading to lovely metallic antique colors in the fall. A strong robust plant with excellent dark-green foliage and sometimes massive flowerheads. Good in acid or alkaline soils and a tough, wind-hardy plant. Grows to 5 ft. (1.5 m).

'**Madame Plumecoq**' Without a doubt my favorite pink hydrangea. How could you not love this soft pink, a truly feminine shade rather than the usual harsh rosy colors so often described as pink. The heads are big, blowsy, dense and look almost edible. Even the leaves look lush as lettuce, so distinctive that this is one the few hydrangeas that can be recognized by leaf alone. To my eye, its only drawback is that the blooms turn an unflattering puce in acid soils, although many of our garden visitors disagree with me. Grows to 5 ft. (1.5 m).

Hydrangea macrophylla
'Madame Truffaut'

'**Madame Truffaut**' has beautiful soft powder-blue mophead flowers. The outer sepals are smooth edged and clean, with a second double frilled flower within. Florets are frilly edged or serrated and sit very flat, giving the impression that all four florets are joined into one star-shaped flower. In early spring the outer sepals are blue while the inner ones are creamy-white, which is a delightful contrast. Has pale leaves and a weak constitution when young and should be grown in the shade. 5 ft. (1.5 m).

'**Maréchal Foch**' An old variety with winning ways. Often used as an indoor plant because it's a good blue and is an easy plant to force into flower out of season. In the garden it is one of the best blues, but it does take a few seasons to show us the good colors. It's also a very attractive plant as a pink mophead. It is remontant, flowering on laterals as well as terminals and thus a mass bloomer. The flowers have a very clean appearance with smooth sepals and tight, round heads that dry very successfully. It forms a small to medium-sized shrub (3–7 ft. or 1–2 m).

'Mariesii' This is the original plant collected in Japan by Charles Maries in 1879 and used in the early breeding programs to give us the cultivars we enjoy today. The early offspring were cultivars such as 'Blue Wave', 'White Wave', and 'Lilacina'. 'Mariesii' itself is usually a good clean soft pink, with blue true flowers, or sometimes it's white with just a hint of pink. It's a tough hardy plant growing to 7 ft. (2 m).

'Masja' A terrific little potted plant because it has rich healthy foliage topped with glowing red blooms. Ideal for tubs and raised beds, but also a very good garden plant growing around waist high. When the red mops fade they often take on a metallic antique color. Popular with cut flower growers. 4 ft. (1.2 m).

'Mathilda Gutges' One of the best blues with fabulous cobalt-blue heads. It needs an acid soil to perform well as it's muddy pink in alkaline soil. A very good foliage plant with rich blackish-green leaves. It's a perfect plant for small gardens, for tubs and as an indoor potted plant. Forms a compact bush to 4 ft. (1.2 m).

'Merritt's Supreme' has long been one of my favorites. It performs well in any soil and any situation. Looks great in shade but handles full sun too. It's a rich purple-blue in acid (pH. 5.5) soil and a pleasing rosy pink in lime. The big bold heads are held aloft on thick chunky stems and can be cut for indoor decoration. In autumn the colors change to maroon or gun-metal blue and make terrific dried flowers. Grows to 5 ft. (1.5 m).

TOP: *Hydrangea macrophylla* 'Masja'

ABOVE: *Hydrangea macrophylla* 'Mathilda Gutges'

LEFT: *Hydrangea macrophylla* 'Merritt's Supreme' in the foreground.

Hydrangea macrophylla
'Merveille Sanguine'

'**Merveille Sanguine**' For me this is the most fascinating and unusual of all the macrophylla cultivars. Everyone loves this plant, with its rich dark chocolate foliage and luscious mophead flowers that start out a glowing blood-red and gradually turn to wine-purple. It's a branch sport from 'Merveille', meaning "marvelous," and appropriately "sanguine" means "blood." For a while I anglicized the name as "marvelous blood," until I thought to switch the words around to call it "Bloody Marvelous." Others have changed the name to 'Raspberry Crush' and 'Brunette'. Whatever the name, this plant is so different you won't confuse it with any other hydrangea. In some cooler parts of the world the shrub does seem a little tender and is inclined to sulk, but for many of us it's the most exciting plant in the garden. It makes a wonderful cut flower and has been taken up in recent times by commercial flower growers. Grows to 5 ft. (1.5 m).

You could grow straight 'Merveille' with nice rounded pinky red mops, but why would you bother when this sport is so much better?

'**Miss Belgium**' A strong rosy pink in alkaline soil or in containers. A perfect plant for pots and tubs as it stays small and compact. Laden with small mophead flowers, but often the stems are rather weak. Not the best plant for acid soils as the flowers will be a strident purple-blue. 3 ft. (1 m).

'**Montgomery**' is a great garden plant providing a variety of colors depending on the acidity of the soil. The pleasing thing is that it looks pretty whatever the pH of the soil. In acid soils the purple-magenta flowers have a retina-vibrating blue luster in the center. The flowers can vary from rich ruby-red in alkaline soil to beetroot-purple and maroon in strongly acid gardens. Clean flat flowers give the impression of being fused together to form a complete ball in modest sized heads. In the fall, these heads take on exciting red and purple colors. It is reasonably sun-tolerant, which is good for creating dried flowers. A small to medium-sized shrub, 4 ft. (1.3 m) '**Holehird Purple**' is very similar.

LEFT: Hydrangea macrophylla 'Miss Belgium'

BELOW: Hydrangea macrophylla 'Montgomery'

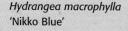

Hydrangea macrophylla
'Nigra'

'**Mrs. W.J. Hepburn**', sometimes known as 'Miss Hepburn', is an old variety bred in the 1920s, but it's still worthy of a place in the garden for the large dense mop flowers in deep pink. These later take on nice antique colors. The plant is strong and has bold healthy leaves. Grows to 4 ft. (1.2 m).

'**Nightingale**' (syn. '**Nachtigall**') My favorite blue lacecap. Forms a tall upright bush with rich green foliage topped in cornflower-blue lacecaps. Each flower has a clean smooth appearance as if manicured. The bush even looks good in winter with a mass of strong yellow stems. Ideal for planting in drifts in shady dells, but it will handle full sun and wind as well as coastal climates. It grows to 5 ft. (1.5 m).

'**Nigra**' An old Chinese cultivar first introduced as *H. mandshurica*, a name still used occasionally. There is only one reason to grow this bush and that is the shiny black stems. The flowers are small rounded mopheads that can be a delicate pink or soft blue. More often the flowers seem to be a muddy color or a harsh purple.

The bush grows to 5 ft. (1.5 m). If grown vigorously to ensure strong black stems, then it has some garden merit, but I am sure it will soon be superseded by new black-stemmed varieties with better flower and stem color.

'**Nikko Blue**' In some ways this is the standard against which other blues are measured. Hugely popular and deservedly so for the smooth round mops of pale blue heads. It can be a passable pink in lime soils. It's very floriferous and produces new flower stems throughout the summer. Popular in cold districts because it is remontant, but equally happy in hot summer climes too. Forms a modest-sized bush of 5 ft. (1.5 m). There do seem to be different forms of this around, though they all have the pale blue mops.

Hydrangea macrophylla
'Nikko Blue'

'Oregon Pride' A sport from 'Merritt's Supreme', with shiny black stems and delightful maroony mophead flowers. Grows to 5 ft. (1.5 m).

'Otaksa' is an old Japanese cultivar named by Philipp von Siebold after a Japanese girl, O-taki-san or Miss Taki. Forms a big bold plant with massive flowerheads. Ideal for windy coastal gardens and also as a backdrop or hedge. I like them for the huge dried flowers they provide. The flowers turn the palest shade of green in fall and are perfect for drying. In summer the enormous creamy flowers have the faintest shade of flax blue in acid soils and the softest hint of pink in alkaline ones. The plant and the flowers are surprisingly sun-tolerant. 8 ft. (2.5 m).

Hydrangea macrophylla
'Otaksa'

'**Paris**' One of the new 'City Line' series. Ideal as a potted plant and an excellent low-growing mophead for gardens. I have to say this is the reddest red I've ever seen, and it positively glows. Does manage better than most to keep the red color in an acid soil, and for this I rate it highly. The flowers can be huge on a well-fed plant. The only thing I don't like is the name, for a previous cultivar was named 'Paris' back in the 1920s, and as this is still available it leads to all sorts of confusion.

'**Parzifal**' I love this variety, though it is very changeable. Even the name is inconstant, appearing as 'Parsifal' and 'Parsival' as well as 'Parzival'. Tight round heads are made up of frilly, starry florets creating a very different flower to the typical smooth or rounded mopheads. The colors too, are novel and exciting as it often bears three different-colored heads at the one time. Perfect in any soil as it's rosy pink in lime and in acid conditions it is common to see pink, magenta-rose and light sea-blue flowers all on the one bush. In fall the colors antique to rose and purples. Makes wonderful cut flowers and dried material. Best grown in light shade to protect the colors from burning and to maintain flower quality for later cutting. It's a modest bush size (5 ft. or 1.5 m).

'**Passion**' One of the new 'YOU-ME' series from Japan, produced by Ryoji Irie, a plant breeder and rock guitarist from Kyoto. More than a double, each full bloom in rich pink or smoky blue looks more like a miniature rose and helps create a froth of blossom when the bush is in full flower. Each head should antique nicely to shades of green. Suitable for pots and for open gardens. Grows to 3 ft. (1 m).

Hydrangea macrophylla
'Piamina'

'Penny Mac' is named after Penny McHenry, the founder of the American Hydrangea Society. This terrific plant came from her garden and is notable on three counts. Firstly, being a remontant, it is capable of flowering all summer, even after late frosts. Secondly, because it is much more cold hardy than most other cultivars, it's an ideal choice for gardeners in cold regions who want to trial a few macrophylla hydrangeas. Of course it's notable too for reminding us about a special person who did so much to popularize hydrangeas. The mophead flowers are a pleasant pink or mid-blue, depending on your soil. Grows to 5 ft. (1.5 m).

'Pia' (syn. 'Piamina', 'Winning Edge') A true dwarf, rarely exceeding 2 ft. (60 cm). Not only is the plant small but the round heads are in proportion, being very tiny round mops. Because of its dwarf nature the plant is rather weak. Flowers are a pink to pale red in alkaline soil, but a harsh inky color in acid soils. Makes a neat low hedge and also useful as a window box or tub plant where it can be kept pink.

'Pompadour' If you're wanting a really soft pink mophead, this could be the plant for you. The very large heads of pale pink are delicious, almost good

Hydrangea macrophylla
'Princess Juliana'

enough to eat. The sepals have a pretty frilly edge. An ideal choice for containers and if your soil is acid, potted plants will be the only way of obtaining the delicate color. It makes a good cut flower. The bush grows to 7 ft. (2 m), but unfortunately it is prone to mildew.

'Président Doumer' Forms a large rather lax bush with dark serrated leaves and spotty stems. The neat round flowerheads are made up of clean smooth-edged sepals. The colors are stunning, either vibrant red in lime or ruby-red to maroon in acid soil. This hydrangea offers splendid colors in any soil, but has a slightly weak constitution, performing best in warm climates. It grows to 4 ft. (1.2 m).

'Président Touchard' An excellent mophead with masses of smallish flowers in reddish-pink, or a vibrant purple in acid soil. One of my favorite purple flowers. Grows to 5 ft. (1.5 m).

'Princess Beatrix' A genuine pink and not rosy as most pinks turn out to be. The large strong heads are made up of very serrated huge sterile florets. The overall impression is of something frilly and yet rigid and firm. Makes a wonderful cut flower because the heads are so stiff. One of the best pinks for an acid soil, 'Princess Beatrix' is a low-growing bush (4 ft. or 1.2 m) with healthy foliage.

'Princess Juliana' Rich creamy flowers open fully and retain a hint of cream in among the white. Smooth rounded sepals give this mophead a neat, clean appearance and rich dark serrated leaves provide a good contrast. It is a fairly low-growing bush, which makes it ideal for smaller gardens, also for providing dried flowers after they turn pale green in fall. It is reasonably sun-tolerant for a white mophead and grows to 5 ft. (1.5 m).

LEFT: *Hydrangea macrophylla* 'Quadricolor'

ABOVE: *Hydrangea macrophylla* 'Red Emperor' with 'Nikko Blue' in the foreground.

'**Quadricolor**' An unusual variety with four distinct leaf colors: two shades of green (light and dark), creamy-white and vivid yellow. The strong yellow color is on the edges of most of the leaves and is the easy way to distinguish this cultivar from the other variegated hydrangeas. The lacecap flowers, which often appear late in the season and sometimes not at all, are white to very pale pink or blue. A popular plant with flower arrangers. The plant needs protection from sun that burns, cold frosts that kill and slugs that simply love it. Grows to 5 ft. (1.5 m). '**Lemon Wave**' is very similar, except it has more yellow in the leaf.

'**Red Emperor**' One of my favorite reds simply because it's tidy, has neat rounded heads and most of all because it tries to stay red even in acid soil. In very acid soils it will turn ruby red and even magnolia-purple. Of course in alkaline soils the flowers are even better—a rich vivid crimson. Good cut flower with modest-sized tidy mops. It forms a good dense shrub from 4–5 ft. (1.2–1.5 m).

'**Red Star**' This attractive variety vividly demonstrates the changeability of the hydrangea's flower color. Usually described as having a good round-headed red flower, the bush's mopheads turn to an incredibly rich French blue in acid soils, making a nonsense of its name. Grows to 7 ft. (2 m).

TOP: *Hydrangea macrophylla* 'Romance'

ABOVE: *Hydrangea macrophylla* 'Romance', blue

ABOVE RIGHT: *Hydrangea macrophylla* 'Renate Steiniger'

'**Renate Steiniger**' A beautiful hybrid, forming a modest-sized bush. The clean, rounded mopheads are one of the best blues. Fall colors include crimson, green and metallic blues. Destined to become a standard for everyone wanting a top blue, this hydrangea has the merit of achieving its rich color very quickly, whereas some blues take two or three years to reach this result. It is reasonably hardy and can be used in pots and tubs. Grows 4–5 ft. (1.2–1.5 m).

'**Rheinland**' (syn. '**Red Glow**') An old variety, but still one of the best reds. Goes purple in acid soil. The vibrant-toned mopheads are ideal for cut flowers. Good as a potted plant, growing to 5 ft. (1.5 m).

'**Ripple**' is an eye-catching new hybrid. Initially it looks red, but the spiraled sepals are really green to white and strongly etched in red, creating a glorious two-toned effect. The flowers are held in a tight mophead and as they open become more candy pink while still keeping the intense red edges. Bred by Mototeru Yatabe in Japan. Grows to 3 ft. (1 m).

'**Romance**' has spectacular starry double flowers in two tones of pink. Looks handsome as a blue in acid soil. The head is full like a mophead, but somehow flatter like a lacecap. Another from the new 'YOU-ME' series created by Ryoji Irie in Kyoto, Japan, it grows to 3 ft. (1 m).

'Rotschwanz' (syn. 'Redstart') A fabulous Teller lacecap with long ray florets that are fluted and twirled like a propeller. The flower color is remarkable too, with rich red wine sterile florets and two-toned white and red true flowers. In the fall the colors become even more vivid. A strong healthy shrub plant with lush "good enough to eat" leaves and even has fall-colored leaves. Grows to 4 ft. (1.2 m).

'Satellite' has carmine-red to deep crimson mopheads. It is one of the best red varieties, with compact rounded heads that look fantastic all summer, on a tough healthy plant deserving of better recognition. It grows to 4 ft. (1.2 m).

'Seafoam' Thought by some to be the wild form of *H. macrophylla*, this is sometimes called *H. maritima* 'Seafoam' referring to the maritime or coastal habitat of the original wild plants. The name was proposed by Michael Haworth Booth, who remained convinced the macrophylla hydrangeas were all hybrids. As the name suggests, 'Seafoam' is quite happy growing near the sea and has large glossy leaves that seem to cope quite happily with the littoral. The bold lacecap flowers, pleasantly scented, can be 12 in. (30 cm) wide. Large white sterile florets surround the mass of lilac-mauve to blue fertile flowers. This tall plant will grow to 7 ft. (2 m) and tolerates full sun, shade and wind, including salt wind. Brilliant for planting in large drifts under trees.

TOP: *Hydrangea macrophylla* 'Seafoam'

BELOW LEFT: *Hydrangea macrophylla* 'Rheinland'

BELOW: *Hydrangea macrophylla* 'Rotschwanz'

BOTTOM: *Hydrangea macrophylla* 'Ripple'

Hydrangea macrophylla
'Shamrock'

'**Shamrock**' was selected and named by Corinne Mallet of the famed Shamrock hydrangea collection in Varengeville sur Mer, near Dieppe in France. This superb garden has the largest collection of hydrangeas in the world. 'Shamrock' the cultivar has a delightful Japanese air, with delicious double florets surrounding the fertile flowers in true lacecap fashion. Heads emerge silver-pink, turning deeper pink to red as summer rolls on, and can even be violet in acid ground. 'Shamrock' has the great advantage of being hardier to cold than many other Japanese-style hydrangeas. Grows to 5 ft. (1.5 m).

'**Sir Joseph Banks**' is no longer a popular buy, but it does have some interesting qualities. It's a big old-fashioned variety with enormous mops of white or the palest pink/blue, depending on the soil. Best grown in coastal regions as it tolerates the fiercest of gales, but is prone to frost inland. It grows to 10 ft. (3 m). It is really only of value as a backdrop or for windy sites. Supposedly the original mophead brought from Canton to London for Sir Joseph Banks, who sailed to the Pacific with Captain Cook.

'**Soeur Thérèse**' (syn. '**Sister Thérèse**') A delightful pure white mophead growing to perfection in shade. The flowers tend to scorch in the sun. It has a rather lax open habit because the weight of the flowers tends to bow the stems, but this adds to the charm of the plant. The flowers take on a pleasant pink or even red tinge in fall. Can be frost tender. Originally called 'Petite Soeur Thérèse de l'Enfant Jésus' but mercifully abbreviated now. It grows to 7 ft. (2 m).

'**Sontagskind**' Sometimes known as 'Sunday's Child', the English translation, this is an excellent fairly new dark-red cultivar. Nice tight round heads are well presented above a small bush (3 ft. or 1 m). It's hardy and easy to grow in any region, so seems destined to become one of the standard red varieties.

'**Snowball**' or '**Schneeball**' can be a terrific plant, but it can be awful too, depending on your climate and how much shade you provide. In a shady spot in a moist situation it's a superb white mophead. But when given a site with too much sun, or conditions that are too dry, the flowers could burn in an instant. Having very large heads, sometimes the plant is reluctant to flower. Grows to 7 ft. (2 m).

'**Tokyo Delight**' Pure white sepals surround the soft pink true flowers in a small lacecap. The sterile florets gradually turn pink and eventually a red color in a similar fashion to 'Grayswood' (see page 129). One of the few hydrangeas to have colored leaves in fall, which possibly means it has some *H. serrata* blood. Unfortunately it's very prone to disease. It forms an upright bush to 7 ft. (2 m).

'**Tricolor**' A variegated plant with foliage that is deep green, grayish-green and pale yellow. White sterile flowers have a tinge of pink in a lacecap shape. It is believed to be a sport of *H. m.* 'Mariesii', possibly the first *H. macrophylla* in cultivation. Slugs and snails will devastate the plant if it's not protected, and it needs shade. Can be used to light up a shady area. It grows to 7 ft. (2 m).

LEFT: *Hydrangea macrophylla* 'Westfalen'

ABOVE: *Hydrangea macrophylla* 'Trophy'

'**Trophy**' A beautiful and very unusual hydrangea with huge white lacecaps. The sterile flowers are often double and arranged not just in a simple circle, but appear all across the plate-like flower. Best in a shady spot as it can burn. Grows to 7 ft. (2 m).

'**Veitchii**' This is an old Japanese variety taken to England by Charles Maries for his employer, the Veitch Nursery, and thus the name. Forms a large robust shrub with healthy foliage. The flowers are big flat white lacecaps with sterile sepals in threes, which is unusual (they're usually in fours). The flowers take on a pink and then red tinge in *H. serrata* fashion. Now being used again as a parent in breeding because it is so healthy and frost tolerant. It grows 7 ft. (2 m) high.

'**Venice**' is one of the 'City Line' series, with bright pink round heads turning rich blue in acid soils. Sometimes reluctant to flower, which is unusual for any macrophylla. To keep the pink coloration, grow in containers. It will reach 3 ft. (1 m).

'**Vienna**' is another from the series of 'City Line' cultivars and has a ball of true pink flowers. It makes an excellent potted plant or small shrub for tubs on a deck. Grows to 3 ft. (1 m).

'**Westfalen**' An excellent all-round plant that forms a dense, compact bush with vermilion-red flowers that tend toward crimson in an acid soil. Because of

Hydrangea macrophylla 'White Wave' showing pinky-mauve antique shades.

its compact habit (4 ft. or 1.2 m) and free-flowering nature it looks brilliant in tubs and pots where the pH can be controlled.

'**White Wave**' is an old variety, but still has masses of charm. It's a sister plant to 'Blue Wave' and 'Lilacina', all of them being seedlings of *H. m.* 'Mariesii'. Smothered in pristine pure white lacecaps that gradually take on a pinky-mauve tinge. A good strong plant, 5 ft. (1.5 m) high, or occasionally up to 7 ft. (2 m), 'White Wave' is happy in sun or shade, though in a colder climate it tends to flower better in full sun. It really lights up a dark shady corner.

'**Zaunkönig**' A lovely Swiss Teller lacecap named after the European "wren," a tiny bird with a domed nest. The flat, medium-sized lacecap flowers are deep vivid erythrocyte red in alkaline conditions, or rich sea-lavender violet in acid soils. Scalloped sterile sepals surround the pinky-mauve true flowers and some of the sterile florets are raised above the lacecap, giving a two-tiered effect. It is best in a warm climate and grows to 5 ft. (1.5 m).

H. paniculata

H. paniculata are deservedly popular. They're tough cold-hardy plants, easy to grow and propagate and best of all they are laden with huge snowy blossoms all through the height of summer. Then as fall approaches the blossoms turn pink and it's at this stage they can be cut for indoor decoration. The wild forms have a pointy panicle flower that is a light and airy mix of true and sterile flowers. They look a bit like cones of old-fashioned lace embellishing the bush. Over the years people have selected forms with more sterile florets to create a denser showier head. The extreme example of this is the ever popular "peegee" or *H. paniculata* 'Grandiflora' with its huge dense blooms. Often they are so heavy they weigh down the branches and even break the brittle stems. In recent years we have many more new cultivars available, mostly due to the efforts of (the late) Jelena and Robert de Belder. At their Kalmthout Arboretum in Belgium they created the best collection of *H. paniculata* in the world. Many of the new cultivars they selected are now available to gardeners, and most have a better blend of sterile and fertile flowers keeping the flowerhead in proportion.

H. paniculata are strong, easy-care, long-lived plants. They are hardier than most species, tolerating extremely cold winters down to Zone 4. As a bonus they are not fussy about the soil type as long as the drainage is reasonable. Like most shrubs, they prefer a well-drained, moist soil, but will grow in clay or rocky ground. They will tolerate more drought than the soft *H. macrophylla* types, but that's not to say you should site them in dry places as they do enjoy regular rainfall.

The height of the bush varies depending on the cultivar. Some like *H. p.* 'Floribunda' and 'Grandiflora' can turn into trees. Thankfully, most cultivars are more like 5 to 7 ft. (1.5–2 m) and can be kept in bounds by regular pruning.

A collection of *Hydrangea paniculata* in the author's garden.

Ideally they should be grown in full sun. Choose a sheltered site because the stems are brittle and easily broken by strong winds. Other than storm damage, they are easy-care plants, untouched by diseases or pests, other than deer. A native of Japan and southeast China, *H. paniculata* was first introduced to Western cultivation by Philipp von Siebold. In recent times new forms have come from both China and Japan.

All gardeners love the paniculata types of hydrangea. How could you not appreciate these floriferous white heads of bloom? Old cultivars remain "must haves" on the lists of those whose gardens suit hydrangeas, and the latest introductions are generating renewed interest in this type. Probably the peegee ones

create the most excitement, being pendulous with the sheer heaviness of bloom, whereas other cultivars are light and perky, pointing skyward.

All of the cultivars and clones have flowers in shades of white. How can white vary, you may ask. Well, some begin as creamy-white, maturing to clear cold white and then as fall approaches they finally take on a delectable pink tinge. Others start frosty white and remain that shade all summer until they fade to brown, or sometimes a gentle pale green. Sunlight encourages pink, while shade gives green hues. Often it's the leaf that varies, with the peegee having rather plain, slightly hairy oval leaves while others have tactile hairy leaves and yet others plain smooth green. In the following list the first two forms of *H. paniculata* are particularly notable for their foliage.

H. p.* forma *velutina Never mind the flowers, just touch the leaves. Everyone squirms with delight at the feel of these velvet pads. No surprise then that "velutina" means "hairy." The bush forms an arching airy shrub around 4 ft. (1.2 m) high and tends to be wider. The flowers are long thin triangles of white lace that turn red in fall.

H. p.* forma *viridis "Viridis" means "green," and true enough, this wild form has rich dark-green smooth leaves. As a foliage plant it beats a peegee hands down. The bush is usually tall and very vigorous, growing to 5 ft. (1.5 m) or more. The strong, erect stems are each topped with a yellowy-white cone of sterile and true flowers with a hint of green. Later on the flowers show no inclination to go red as many strains do, but instead take on a delicious shade of green for the antique display.

H. paniculata cultivars

'Barbara' see 'The Swan'

'**Bridal Veil**' Suitable only for large gardens because of the size of the bush, which ultimately grows to over 10 ft. (3 m) high. Blooms are a mix of pure white sterile and true flowers. The sterile flowers have twirl-like "propellers" and can be serrated. The large heavy blooms appear in succession throughout the summer months. Seen as too big and bold by some, and appreciated by others.

'**Brussels Lace**' A very large bush with suitably large lacy blooms that are a mix of sterile and true flowers, possibly a bit too filigreed and sparse for some tastes. All of the flowers appear early in the season and all open at once, creating a top display. Even though the blooms are huge, they tend to keep upright because of the mix of flowers, which generally remain white for the duration of summer. Bred by Robert and Jelena de Belder in Belgium, this cultivar grows to 7 ft. (2 m) or more.

'**Burgundy Lace**' Appropriately named, this large bush to 7 ft. (2 m) has long pointed white lacy flowers that turn pink and then eventually burgundy-red in the fall. A choice de Belder selection and a long-time favorite.

'**Chantilly Lace**' is a selection by U.S. breeder Michael Dirr, chosen because the heads are held aloft on a strong upright plant and because the plant tolerates hot summers. It also has some other winning attributes, notably excellent dark green foliage and long showy panicles with a mix of true and sterile flowers that turn pink in the fall. Grows to 6 ft. (1.8 m).

'**Dharuma**' is a Japanese selection grown as a miniature. Most paniculata clones become huge bushes whereas this tiny plant reaches only 3 ft. (1 m). The flat-topped flowers are a mix of true and sterile white flowers that very quickly turn pink. A novelty plant that is sure to be used for breeding in an effort to create smaller varieties.

'**Floribunda**' One of the first clones to come out of Japan back in the 1800s, this plant forms an absolutely huge bush with masses of very large pointed white blooms containing a mix of true and sterile flowers. All of the latter tend to sit prettily facing outwards from the central cone. Flowers tend to go pink as the summer progresses. As this hydrangea forms such a tall plant, sometimes up to 20 ft. (6 m), it needs fairly drastic pruning each winter to be feasible for a small garden. It looks spectacular in a large garden as an isolated specimen, or at the back of a border.

'**Garnet**' Another de Belder selection, but quite different from most as it has unusual felt-like leaves derived from *H. p.* forma *velutina* in its parentage. A late-flowering bush, it forms a modest-sized shrub 5 ft. (1.5 m) and bears small triangular pointed flowers. The sterile sepals turn pink and almost red. 'Angel's Blush' is similar and is a sister seedling.

Hydrangea paniculata 'Brussels Lace'

'**Grandiflora**' Introduced from Japan by Philipp von Siebold in the 1860s, this is the best known and most popular version of *H. paniculata*. It goes by the common name of "PeeGee" (or "PG"), from its initials. The bush bears huge triangular-shaped heads of sterile flowers that are so heavy the branches bend over with their weight. This adds considerably to the charm of the shrub. Sometimes the branches are so heavy with the weight of the flowers that they break in a strong wind, so—probably more than any other—this form needs good shelter. Flower cones can be up to 18 in. (45 cm) long and 12 in. (30 cm) wide at the base. The blooms are a lovely creamy-white, opening to pure white before turning pinky shades as fall approaches. Flowers can be successfully cut for dried arrangements at that time.

An excellent subject for a mixed border, or as an informal group, this hydrangea can be left to grow into a very large upright shrub to 10 ft. (3 m) or more, or you can drastically prune it every winter to keep the bush within bounds and to increase the size of the flowers. It is also possible to successfully cut 'Grandiflora' to ground level every year in a herbaceous border, as it flowers on new wood. It can be pruned to a standard-type tree form or as a bush, but is probably best grown as a half standard with a strong central trunk to hold the arching stems.

'**Green Spire**' has very long pointy flowers that open almost green, change briefly to white before taking on a green tinge again in the antique phase, especially in part shade. The flowers are a mix of sterile and true and quite charming. Unfortunately it develops into a very big bush, sometimes reaching 20 ft. (6 m), and is only suitable for large gardens.

'**Kyushu**' A lovely dainty form of the species collected on Kyushu Island in Japan by Collingwood Ingram (sometimes known as "Cherry" Ingram for his

love of Japanese flowering cherries). The name "Kyushu" was suggested by his friend Lady Anne Berry. This hydrangea makes a much smaller bush than the species and has smaller heads of flowers in a pointed cone shape. These heads are a mix of sterile and fertile flowers and, being lighter, they remain erect and do not bend the stems at all. The plant's modest 5 ft. (1.5 m) size makes it ideal for smaller gardens and it produces a wonderful contrast when planted with purple or bronze forms of *Acer palmatum*.

'Limelight' (or 'Zwijnenburg', after its breeder, Pieter Zwijnenburg) This offers a novel color break as the unusual flowers open lime green and can remain green for some time, depending on the climate and the amount of shade. Has the potential to produce greenish flowers all summer if grown in a mild climate or in part shade. Its very large heads are packed with heaps of sterile flowers and are thus very good for the vase. Generally the stems are strong enough to maintain these bulky heads, but you may need to summer prune to reduce the weight. Improves with age as the plant builds up strength. Grows to 7 ft. (2 m).

'Little Lamb' (or 'Lammetje') is like a frothy version of 'Grandiflora', having a host of small white flowers. Sometimes it has so many small heads packed together it looks like extra flowers at the base of each head. This very floriferous bush blooms early and becomes a modest-sized plant, between 5 and 6 ft. (1.5–1.8 m) high. If you have a small garden it would be an excellent choice.

'Mount Everest' or 'Everest' Similar to, but stronger than 'Grandiflora'. Good dense heads of white turn pink as summer progresses. Grows tall—15 ft. (5 m)—and has good robust green foliage. Selected from the Hillier Arboretum in England.

ABOVE LEFT: *Hydrangea paniculata* 'Little Lamb'

TOP AND ABOVE: *Hydrangea paniculata* 'Limelight'

ABOVE: *Hydrangea paniculata* 'Quick Fire'

ABOVE RIGHT: *Hydrangea paniculata* 'Unique'

BELOW: *Hydrangea paniculata* 'Pinky Winky'

'Pink Diamond' is deservedly popular. Its main claim to fame is the tendency of the mass of sterile flowers to change to pink during the summer. Most paniculata types tend to go pink as summer wanes, but 'Pink Diamond' starts showing pink tinges almost as soon as the flowers emerge. The very large heads and sterile flowers eventually become more rosy, almost red in color. Plant in a sunny site to enhance the color change. It grows to 7 ft. (2 m) and can be best as a bush or encouraged to develop as a tree form.

'Pinky Winky' Gotta love this name! It's appropriate too, as the flower quickly turns from white to "pinky winky" and even quite a strong red. The panicles are big, showy and glorious in every shade. The plant doesn't get too big (5–6 ft. or 1.5–1.8 m) so it's ideal for suburban gardens. Yet another Belgian cultivar, a variant of 'Pink Diamond'.

'Praecox' is a personal favorite, being such a graceful garden shrub. "Praecox" means "early" and the cones of frothy flowers emerge in early summer. Because the heads are a combination of true and sterile flowers, they are not too heavy and so the bush keeps its upright habit. The flowers are erect, lacy affairs, aerially balanced over a large upright shrub (8 ft. or 2.5 m) with rather dull smooth green leaves. Without a doubt this hydrangea's greatest asset is being first of the season and, like the first strawberries of the year, it is annually delicious. This form was introduced from Japan by Charles Sargent.

'Quick Fire' Another great name for a top plant. This clone flowers really early and so is quick-fire off the mark. Soon the creamy-white heads are turning pink, then red, and so appear like fire, but the distinction is that other clones have only just begun to flower by then, so this plant really extends the display season. Grows 6–7 ft. (1.8–2 m).

'Ruby', also known as 'Angel Blush', is another de Belder cultivar. It has open fluffy blossoms with plenty of true flowers so the heads are lightweight and remain erect. The white flowers turn pink and then ruby-red if conditions are right. Grows to 7 ft. (2 m).

'The Swan', also known as 'Barbara', has enormous white sepals on a large panicle. You've never seen florets as big as these ones, which have great appeal for gardeners and florists alike. The head is a mix of true and sterile flowers. Like most of the *H. paniculata* cultivars, it makes a good cut flower especially when dried in the antique phase. Another fine de Belder selection. Grows 6–7 ft. (1.8–2 m).

'Tardiva' One of the many prized forms of *H. paniculata* available in recent times, and a real gem because it tends to bloom late in the summer, thus extending the flowering season. Each panicle has a tidy, shapely appearance, with the bulk of the sterile flowers near its base. Height 7 ft. (2 m).

'Unique' bears a huge panicle of flowers, even larger than 'Grandiflora'. Masses of sterile flowers are so packed together that the impression is of being full to overflowing. The heads take on a pink or even rusty red appearance late in the season. This shrub grows 10–13 ft. (3–4 m).

'White Moth' has dense heads of sterile flowers, more rounded than most. These can be 12 in. (30 cm) across and so heavy as to weigh down the stems. Yet another classy de Belder selection, the plant improves with age when its branches get stronger. Flowers early and over a long period and even produces new flushes of flower through the summer. Grows to 7 ft. (2 m).

H. quercifolia

H. quercifolia grows wild in the southern states of the eastern United States. There on the slopes of the Appalachians they are often found in quite dense woodland. We gardeners are lucky because the plant will grow in sun or shade. In cooler climes it's happier in sun and in warmer zones it prefers some shade from the hot midday sun. They are quite hardy, being equally happy in cold inland sites and in coastal regions, though best not planted too close to the sea as it is not tolerant of storm winds. The large triangular cones of creamy-white blossoms are reminiscent of *H. paniculata* and like their cousin the flowers appear from midsummer onwards. Like many other hydrangeas, *H. quercifolia* is a wonderful cut flower and useful for drying.

Hydrangea quercifolia 'Snowflake' beginning to take on antique pink shades.

The name "quercifolia" comes from its oak-shaped leaves, which are similar to those of the American red oaks—*Quercus* spp. The big bold leaves turn rich crimson and purple in the fall and they are undoubtedly the best hydrangea for autumn color.

These blazing red and burgundy colors are more likely to appear if the plant is grown in full sun. At this time of year the flowers take on an antique pink coloration that contrasts nicely with the leaf colors.

The plants typically grow around 5 ft. (1.5 m) high and up to 7 ft. (2 m) wide: some may grow even bigger, say around 10–12 ft. (3–3.5 m).

Preferring a good rich, moist, but well-drained soil, *H. quercifolia* tolerates both acid and alkaline soil. Do not plant them in poorly drained conditions or in too dry a site. They can sucker a little, but this is rarely a problem as they don't become rampant and new plants are easily propagated from the suckers.

If it has one drawback, this hydrangea can be attacked by root rot, causing the plant to decline or even die. Otherwise it seems to be free of pests and diseases.

H. quercifolia is hardy down to Zone 5, but they do need warm summers to flower well and to ripen the wood to cope with the upcoming cold winters. While they thrive in warmer areas such as Zones 9 and 10, they often don't perform well in the intermediate Zones 7 and 8. This is possibly a lack of summer heat to ripen the wood.

In a garden they look very much at home in a woodland setting, but also look fine in a mixed border. In cold areas a novel way to grow them is in large tubs.

Hydrangea quercifolia
'Harmony'

H. quercifolia cultivars

'Alice' A Michael Dirr selection with very long showy white blooms containing a mix of sterile and true flowers. Is considered a robust and easy plant to grow as well as being more sun tolerant than most forms. The flowers turn pink with age and contrast nicely with the rich red fall leaf colors. Grows 10–12 ft. (3–3.5 m).

'Alison' is another Michael Dirr seedling with slightly smaller more upright flowers than usual. Their display is enriched by the sizzling red-wine color of the leaves in fall. Grows 10–12 ft. (3–3.5 m).

'Harmony' has huge weighty white blooms like dollops of ice cream, not the usual triangular flowerhead of a typical quercifolia. While the panicles are very showy, they can be so heavy as to pull the branches apart. Grows 10–12 ft. (3–3.5 m).

'John Wayne' has large heads with pretty white ray florets. It is popular because it tolerates hot climates. Good fall color too. Grows 5 ft. (1.5 m).

'Little Honey' is unusual on two counts: the leaves are yellow and the plant is a compact dwarf. It was selected by Englishman Peter Catt from a batch of 'Pee Wee' plants, so the flower and fall leaf are the same as this variety. Grows to 3 ft. (1 m).

'Pee Wee' is a neat miniature form just perfect for small gardens. The flower size is small too, in keeping with the plant, and usually the dense white heads are about 4 in. (10 cm) long. Grows to 3 ft. (1 m).

'Sike's Dwarf' is another great plant for small gardens. Has larger heads than 'Pee Wee', with a mix of true and sterile flowers. Good fall colors. Grows to 4 ft. (1.2 m).

'Snowflake' is a superb double-flowered form. In fact, the spirals of sterile flowers make this almost a quadruple flower. Each floret pirouettes, forming a perfect spiral. Not only is the flower a great improvement, but the plant has a better constitution than the straight species and becomes a much better shaped bush. Its arching full form creates a dense rounded dome of superb foliage topped by fascinatingly beautiful blooms. This hydrangea provides interest almost all year round. The fabulous white double flowers change to rosy pink and even look good when dried in the winter. Fall colors are superb, being a combination of wine-red to maroon, with brighter reds and orange for good

measure. It is a plant that looks good combined with other shrubs or perennials, but is also attractive enough to be a garden focal point. Has the ability to look brilliant close up and equally stunning from twenty paces away.

As with the species, it needs warm summers to thrive. It's in my personal top ten garden plants.

'**Snow Queen**' is notable as a very showy single-flower form. The individual creamy-white flowers are much larger than those of the species and seem to present themselves on one plane, creating a perfect cone of white. The leaves are slightly reflexed and this adds to the clean appearance of the bush, making it without a doubt my favorite single-flowered quercifolia. The blooms take on delightful pink tinges and then there's the bonus of the exceptional fall color. Not so happy in very hot climates, but the perfect plant for semi-shade or cooler regions. Grows to 6 ft. (1.8 m).

'**Tennessee**' has large cones of blossom with the sterile florets spaced neatly among the true flowers. Raised from seed collected in Tennessee by the de Belders, this shrub grows 5–6 ft. (1.5–1.8 m).

H. serrata

This lovely hydrangea hails from Japan and Korea where it is found in woods and forests and often in the cooler mountain areas. *Hydrangea serrata* types similar to *H. macrophylla* and can be used in much the same way. However they are not quite as robust and tolerant of windy or hot and dry situations because the flowers will crisp and dehydrate. In general, *H. serrata* plants are therefore not happy in hot or dry regions, but they tolerate most soils, as long as they are not too alkaline, nor too wet.

Compared to macrophylla types, these serrata shrubs have thinner stems, narrow, often hairy leaves and form a smaller bush. Being smaller than the *H. macrophylla* makes them more suitable for suburban gardens. The name indicates quite accurately that this species has leaves with a jagged edge like a serrated knife, but there again, so do most of the other species.

Some of these hydrangeas have a delightful habit of making three or four color changes per season, meaning your summer garden will never be boring. Some of these, such as 'Glyn Church' and 'Preziosa', go through these same color changes regardless of the acidity of the soil and so they are more predictable than the macrophyllas. If you have a shady spot, these color changes will captivate you all through summer.

The species has flattened lacecap flowers with white, pink or blue ray florets or sterile flowers surrounding blue or white true flowers in the center of the head.

Hardy to Zone 6, this hydrangea is reasonably tolerant of frosts. Pests and diseases are few and far between, powdery mildew being the only one of any consequence.

There are some remarkable forms and hybrids of *H. serrata* that are worth procuring.

H. s. forma *acuminata* has delectable soft hairy leaves with an exaggerated point at the tip. In the wild these plants grow wider than they are tall, creating a bush just over 3 ft. (1 m) high. Pretty lacecap flowers appear in early summer with sterile white or off-white sepals surrounding pink or gray-mauve true flowers. A lovely bush for a shady dell.

'Blue Billow' is a valuable plant for cold hardiness and also bears an attractive blue lacecap flower. Grows to 3 ft. (1 m).

'Blue Bird' has manicured lacecaps in a novel shade of blue. The larger petals are smooth and rounded and arranged in a cross fashion. These are actually closer to white, but the impression of the lacecap is blue because the dome of true flowers within is a heavenly rich blue. The tidy structure of the flower adds to the charm of this plant. It's hard to beat for color, long flowering season, hardiness and grace. Just to top it off, 'Blue Bird' is one of the few hydrangeas with fall leaf color, turning red in late summer. It grows to 4 ft. (1.2 m) and is best in some shade.

'Blue Deckle' is simply irresistible. A light airy bush decked in the softest pale blue lacecap flowers is irresistible. The flowers seem to float above the bush like butterflies. Close up, you can see the deckle-edged sepals in soft powder blue surrounding the pale blue true flowers. Oddly enough, the plant

ABOVE: *Hydrangea serrata* 'Diadem'

RIGHT: *Hydrangea serrata* 'Blue Deckle'

sometimes produces lots of flowers with smooth-edged sepals, thus mocking the name "deckle."

Ideal for small gardens and even for pots, but it also looks marvelous in drifts in larger gardens. Grows best in just a hint of shade. This variety was raised by Michael Haworth-Booth. It grows to 3 ft. (1 m).

'**Diadem**' is a pale blue lacecap ideal for small gardens as it stays low and compact. Its most winning attribute is flowering before virtually any other hydrangea in early summer. Just like summer fruit, the first flowers of the season are extra delicious, but if you want value for money, choose 'Blue Deckle' instead. Grows to 3 ft. (1 m).

'**Glyn Church**' First up, I have to confess I'm not altogether happy with the name of this plant and in my defense I can honestly say tagging it thus was not my idea. I sent some hydrangeas to Corinne Mallet, who owns the fabulous Shamrock collection in Varengeville sur Mer on the French coast near Dieppe, and Corinne labeled these plants as Glyn Church. She soon became so excited about this particular plant that she wanted a name for it and suggested using mine. I, in turn, suggested turning my name into French using "L'église" for Church and "Vallée" for Glyn, but Corinne insisted on retaining the English. Anyway, on to the plant, which is much more exciting than the name. It's a *H. serrata* type with small creamy mopheads opening to pure white. Ideally the plant should be in a morsel of shade, but still get enough sunlight to make the heads change color, which they do in fascinating fashion. First they emerge a rich cream, then fully open to pure white before taking on a pinky tinge. The most remarkable change is still to come when the heads turn a true red and then finally a rich red-wine color. If the plant is grown in a very shady place the flowers turn green in fall and make attractive antique dried flowers.

Apart from its unique coloring, this plant has several valuable talents. It's a remontant variety, so it keeps producing new flowerheads throughout the season, even in colder regions where late frosts can kill the flower buds on most other hydrangeas.

Being a *H. serrata*, the shrub is much hardier than a typical mophead of *H. macrophylla* and is proving to be very cold and heat tolerant. However, like most of the serrata types, it does prefer a bit of shade, especially from the hot midday sun. While sunlight encourages the blooms to undergo the sequence of color changes that are such a feature, too much hot sun will simply burn the flowers and ruin the display. Lime or alkaline soil has no effect on the flower color, a great advantage for gardeners and a good selling point for propagators. Fine in pots as it has a slightly arching, weeping habit, the plant grows 3–5 ft. (1–1.5 m) high and often wider.

'**Golden Sunlight**' has distinct yellow leaves in the spring flush, but they soon fade to green. The flowers are unexceptional white to pink lacecap. Grows to 3 ft. (1 m).

'**Grayswood**' is a wondrous hydrangea. The first impression is of a delicate-looking plant with pale pointy leaves and spotty stems, but appearances are deceptive as it is really quite robust and frost-hardy. Undoubtedly, the highlight is its clean white lacecap, which changes to soft pink, then rose color and finally the color of red wine. The plant needs sunlight to encourage all these color changes, and the bush can exhibit a multitude of shades at any one time. The changing flower colors are enhanced by sunlight, but too much sun and the flowers simply burn. Inside the circle of mutating colors is a dome of smoky-purple true flowers, creating a fascinating contrast. Like many of the serrata types, 'Grayswood' needs a bit more attention than the average hydrangea. If you feed and mulch regularly, it will repay you with lush green leaves and better flowers. Grows to 5 ft. (1.5 m).

'**Kiyosumi**' Although fairly new to Western gardens, this unusual Japanese cultivar has a certain magnetism. The leaves are small, pointed and often tinged with red or bronze, and on first glance don't look like those of any other hydrangea. Although creating a striking upright bush, the plant does tend to be a bit spindly and it pays to prune it to shape every winter to try to make it more compact and dense. The small white lacecap flowers have a red picotee edge, as if the fairies have painted each and every bloom. Can be a bit tricky to grow, for it needs good drainage, some shade and possibly even a stake or cane in the early years. Discovered on Mt. Kiyosumi in 1950, it grows to 6 ft. (1.8 m).

'**Komachi**' (syn. '**Pretty Maiden**') is an unusual form of serrata with almost mophead flowers. The heads are often slightly lopsided and full of double starry

TOP: *Hydrangea serrata* 'Glyn Church'

ABOVE: *Hydrangea serrata* 'Kiyosumi'

TOP: *Hydrangea serrata* 'Miranda'

ABOVE: *Hydrangea serrata* 'Miyama-yae-Murasaki'

flowers. The color varies from pink through lavender to a delicious shade of purple-mauve. Like most serrata types, it's best grown in shade and eventually attains around 3 ft. (1 m).

'Miranda' A beautiful little plant with rich butterfly-blue lacecaps. Both the outer sterile florets and inner true flowers are the same color; combined with the smooth and rounded sepals this makes for a neat and tidy appearance. Being a genuine dwarf plant we can use it for fronting borders and in pots and tubs. The bush grows wider than it does high, creating a low mound with rather pale long pointed leaves. Grows to only 24 in. (60 cm) high.

'Miyama-yae-Murasaki' (syn. 'Purple Tiers') A fabulous form with soft green leaves and beautiful rich dark-blue flowers. Not only are these a superb color but they're arranged in a neat double form, making the lacecaps look even more lacy. Luckily, being a serrata type, it is not overly affected by soil type and while it can be anemic purple in some conditions, or even a muddy pink, nine times out of ten it is a breathtaking blue. The shrub itself can be a little spindly and has an upright habit. Like most serrata types, it prefers shade, especially from the hot midday sun. Grows to 4 ft. (1.2 m).

'Preziosa' is a fabulous hydrangea. The mop flowers are constantly changing color, opening first as pale green, quickly changing to yellow, then cream and finally white before developing pink tinges and spots, becoming totally pink, cherry red and finally red wine. Even better from a gardener's perspective, these color changes happen regardless of the soil pH and so everyone can achieve the same result.

The plant is a little more demanding than most hydrangeas. To perform at its best it needs to be in a well-drained situation in light shade. Too much shade and the flowers won't turn red as it's sunlight that initiates the changes. Too much sun and the flowers will simply burn. A mulch will help keep the flowers pumped with enough moisture to prevent burning.

'Preziosa' is a hybrid with lots of *H. serrata* blood as shown by the leaves tinged with red. It forms an upright shrub, 5 ft. (1.5 m) high, with distinct reddish stems, rather thin and delicate, and slightly red-hued leaves. If 'Preziosa' has a fault, it does sometimes suffer from mildew.

'Shichidanka' is a delightful pink double lacecap with flowers like stars suspended on a wheel. Can tend to lavender and even blue on occasions. Has the added bonus of orangey-red fall colors in the leaves. Grows to 3 ft. (1 m).

'Shirofuji' forms a neat small rounded bush covered in starry white lacecap flowers like a dusting of snow. These double white florets surround the true flowers, exaggerating the snowy appearance and thus inspiring its name, which means "snow-capped Fuji mountain." Grows to 4 ft. (1.2 m).

'Shirotae' is a neat little plant with a narrow leaf form, and seems able to fit in virtually any garden, no matter how small. It bears beautiful double white

Hydrangea serrata
'Preziosa'

starry flowers surrounding the fertile flowers in typical lacecap fashion. As the flowers fade they take on new exciting hues of green in shade or red in sunlight, and sometimes a lovely combination of the two. Unfortunately the plant can be weak and the leaves do tend to look a bit pale, so the bush will benefit from some long-term fertilizer. Grows to 3 ft. (1 m).

'**Tiara**' is a delightful low bush, selected by Maurice Foster. The domed lace-caps can be pink or blue and often turn red or green in the fall. The foliage too changes color, sometimes showing hints of red or even black. Grows to about 3–4 ft. (just over 1 m).

'**Wryneck**' is named after a shy European woodpecker. It forms a small tidy plant with huge soft green leaves. The small round heads of soft blue are so packed with flowers they look cluttered, and often the heads bow with the weight of bloom. This is a novelty plant that takes some years to establish. Grows to 3 ft. (1 m).

Rare and Climbing Hydrangeas

Rare hydrangeas

Hydrangea heteromalla

This hydrangea, very similar to *H. aspera* both in looks and from a cultivation perspective, can be very tall and elegant, but many forms are rather dull and boring. If you wish to buy one, make sure it's an exciting form. The variability is because many are grown from seed and it depends on the source. Some have small dry hairy leaves and a few lacecaps scattered across the top of a sparse open shrub. Others have exciting spear-like foliage, clothed to the ground, and intriguing pink, mauve or white lacecap flowers. Usually the sterile flowers of the lacecap are white or pink surrounding off-white to green true flowers. Some even have flowers in tiers of multiple lacecaps up to an enormous 24 in. (60 cm) wide. These multiple heads can consist of up to eight lacecaps in one huge flower. Most forms are really only suitable for large gardens or parks as they can eventually reach around 16 ft. (5.5 m). Coming originally from Western China and the Himalayas, *H. heteromalla* is reasonably hardy, growing to Zone 6, though some of the larger-leaved forms with huge flowers are very frost-tender and need Zones 9 to 10. This hydrangea is happy in sun or part shade and is rarely attacked by pests or fungi.

RIGHT: *Hydrangea heteromalla*

LEFT: *Hydrangea indochinensis*

FAR LEFT: *Hydrangea longifolia*

H. indochinensis

Fairly new to cultivation, several forms of this frost-tender species have been collected in Vietnam and China in recent times. They vary considerably. Some are rather fragile upright plants with shiny blackish-green pointed leaves and a purple reverse. Others are tidy rounded bushes more like *H. scandens* subsp. *chinensis*. The sterile lacecap flowers are white, sometimes with a hint of pale lilac, while the true flowers are usually an intense purple or blue. It is probably hardy only in Zones 9 and 10.

H. involucrata

An unusual shrub with bristly or hairy leaves and stems. The lacecap flowers open from round buds and have white sterile florets surrounding pretty mauve-colored true flowers. Unfortunately it's hard to come by and even harder to grow. This is a collector's item from Japan and Taiwan. 3 ft. (1 m). Hardy to Zone 7.

H. i. 'Hortensis'

Beautiful but temperamental describes this unusual plant. The semi-double flowers in the palest opaque pink will entrance you, but the poor constitution and weak nature of the plant will make you despair. It is, however, worth persevering for the frilly pastel pink flowers. Hardy to Zone 7.

H. longifolia

Initially an upright bush, to 6 ft. (1.8 m) and arching only with weight and age, this species is noted for very long pointed leaves with a furry texture, and strange round flower buds at the tip of each stem. These seem to take an age to open to a dome of pink true flowers surrounded by white lacecaps. The flowers appear throughout the year in a mild climate, but are concentrated in the fall in cooler regions. The bush is evergreen in warmer climes. Hardy to Zone 8.

Hydrangea scandens subsp. *chinensis* (above) and *Hydrangea scandens* (right) in the author's garden.

H. scandens and *H. s.* subsp. *chinensis*

These rare plants come from southeast China and Taiwan. Sometimes they form a tidy 3 ft. (1 m) shrub but other forms are open and rangy, growing up to 6 ft. (1.8 m) high and wide. The delightful white lacecaps show up splendidly against the dark foliage. Plants are variable when grown from wild collected seed. The leaves range from smooth and hard to soft and hairy, but always with a serrated edge. Some forms are evergreen in a warm climate. Happy in sun or shade, these hydrangeas need a warm spot in a colder climate and are probably hardy only to Zone 7.

Climbing hydrangeas

H. anomala subsp. *petiolaris*

A deciduous climber that is really hardy down to Zone 4, and not too fussy about soil conditions, *H. petiolaris* can be used in a multitude of ways. It looks fantastic climbing up a tree as it clothes the entire trunk, surrounding it with white lacecap flowers in early summer. As it is happy in full sun or shade, *H. petiolaris* can be used to cover unsightly walls, fences and sheds. The roots do cling like ivy, so be aware they may cause you problems if you want to paint the surface. I've seen this climbing hydrangea used to great effect on the outsides of city houses and hotels, on old limestone farm walls or even as a ground cover.

When planting these climbers to ascend trees, take heed—like most climbers, they will grow as high as they can. If given a 7 ft. (2 m) fence, they will climb 7 ft. and then flower. If given a 70 ft. (20 m) tree to climb, they will grow to the full height and take much longer to bloom and most of the flowers will be near the top! This same habit is true of most climbers, so when people say, "Don't grow such and such, it grows 70 ft. high," bear in mind this is only because the plant has been given a 70 ft. tree to climb.

The leaves of this climber are bright and shiny, a rich dark green; its flowers are typical hydrangea lacecaps with large white sterile sepals surrounding the small white true flowers in the central dome. Even the trunks are attractive as the older stems have peeling brown paper-like shedding bark. Initially the climber seems slow to establish and the stems cling tightly to brick or timber, but eventually the plant gets moving and in the second phase will produce horizontal stems extending 12 in. (30 cm) or so from the clinging structural trunks. These horizontal stems are the ones to carry the flowers. The plant needs to be trimmed away from windows, but otherwise does not need regular pruning. Luckily no pests or diseases bother it and you'll have a marvelous climber for life once it has become established.

There is a variegated form of this climber called 'Firefly', with pale yellow margins to the leaf, but it's hard to beat the real thing. Cultivars are hard to find. 'Skylands Giant' is one; it is notable for its large flowers.

H. seemannii

A rare climber from Mexico, *H. seemannii* needs a warm Zone 8 or 9 climate, free of major frosts. (Note that it is generally easier to keep climbers free from frost as they grow vertically and often get the benefit of the warmth from a wall. Buildings give off heat at night and thus also help reduce the effects of frost.) The best thing about this plant is the dark-green glossy evergreen foliage. Flowers are an untidy white lacecap. A collector's plant, *H. seemannii* tends to bloom best in warm climates.

H. serratifolia

A vigorous evergreen climber from Chile and Argentina, this is another that prefers a warm Zone 8 or 9 climate and needs heat to bloom well and keep off frosts. It displays bundles of fluffy white fertile flowers and is quite showy in a warm climate.

The name "serratifolia" doesn't fit, as mostly the leaves are smooth edged.

Some climbing relatives

Decumaria barbara

A semi-evergreen climber from the southern Appalachian Mountains in the United States, this has clinging roots like climbing hydrangeas. Like them, it will grow in shade but tends to flower better if given some sunlight. It has corymbs of white, all true flowers. It is hardy to Zone 8.

Decumaria sinensis

This Chinese version of *Decumaria* is truly evergreen. Its small white flowers in early summer are deliciously scented. It is hardy to Zone 8.

Pileostegia viburnoides

A super evergreen climber that ascends using sucker roots to cling to tree trunks and walls. The thick fleshy leaves are very handsome and are very dark green. It's worth growing this plant for the foliage alone, but you will have to be patient because it's rather slow to establish. The flowers are very small creamy-white cups attached in masses along a thin spike. These thin spikes of flowers are always in threes like a tripod. It will grow in difficult shady places as long as the soil is rich and well drained. One of the very few frost-hardy evergreen climbers for Western gardens, it was introduced by E.H. Wilson in 1908, from Khasia Hills, India. It is hardy to Zone 7 or 8.

Schizophragma hydrangeoides

This species is a relative of hydrangeas, and from a gardener's perspective they're the same. With typical wild hydrangea lacecap flowers decorating the vine, you'd be forgiven for thinking it was another hydrangea. They are very similar to *H. anomala* subsp. *petiolaris*, having the same ivy-like roots. The major differences are that *S. hydrangeoides* has larger flowers and rougher veined leaves. This *Schizophragma* sp. clings with the same ivy-like roots as *H. a.* subsp. *petiolaris*, the only obvious difference being the rougher veined leaves and larger flowers. The latter can be the size of small plates and consist of showy, cream-colored heads. The heart-shaped leaves have a reddish tinge to the outside serrated edges. Content in sun or shade, though it flowers best in sun and is tolerant of hot summers, this frost-hardy deciduous climber is happy down to Zone 5. It hails from Japan.

S. hydrangeoides forma 'Roseum' is a pretty form with rosy-colored bracts.

Schizophragma integrifolium

This Chinese species is a little less frost-hardy than the above, tolerating only Zones 7 to 10. The grayish furry leaves are heart-shaped and the creamy-white lacecaps can be huge, up 12 in. (30 cm wide). The plant has fewer flowers to compensate for the enormous size of each bloom. It is happy in long hot summers. *S. i.* subsp. *faurei* from Taiwan has very tactile furry gray leaves and smaller cream flowers.

Some interesting relatives
Dichroa febrifuga

A widespread and variable plant growing throughout the Himalayas, this tends to form an upright shrub just over 3 ft. (1 m). The leaves are narrow, dull green and slightly hairy, giving the plant a dry, hard-done-by appearance. Not even the flowers bring it to life, as the small round heads of pale blue blossom are intriguing rather than beautiful. They can be slightly pinky in alkaline soil. These are followed by purple berries. This species is quite drought tolerant and seems very accepting of shady conditions, but is not particularly hardy, say around Zone 8.

Pileostegia viburnoides

Dichroa hirsuta

A rangy, rather leggy plant with narrow shiny green leaves. The flowers are loose and pale blue-gray followed by beautiful blue berries, which are without doubt the highlight. This plant is tender as it comes from Vietnam. Grows to around 5 ft. (1.5 m).

Dichroa versicolor

An unusual evergreen relative of the hydrangea, this is originally from North Burma but a quite recent introduction to cultivation. It forms a bold shrub with large glossy leaves, very similar in shape and size to those of *H. macrophylla* but a richer, darker green. It has an upright form, growing 7 ft. (2 m) high and a little less wide. The overall effect is a tropical-looking plant, and yet it is proving surprisingly frost-hardy for some people and has even more chance of survival if given a little shade and shelter. The kind of late frosts that ruin the flower buds of magnolias and rhododendrons leave this shrub untouched. However, the best is still to come as the rich denim-blue flowers are produced more or less all year round.

D. versicolor is a simply stunning plant that I'm sure will become very popular in time. It will grow at the water's edge, tolerating quite wet conditions, and also contends with shade and even drought, although it does not do the plant credit when conditions are too dry. It seems the flower color is unaffected by acidity, unlike its hydrangea relatives.

Over the last few years I have been hybridizing dichroas and getting some interesting results. Some have intense blue berries lasting long into winter. Generally the hybrids have better foliage and a tidier plant habit than the species.

Dichroa versicolor

Appendix I: Hardy varieties of *H. macrophylla* and *H. serrata*

'All Summer Beauty' (M)
'Ami Pasquier' (M)
'Bluebird' (S)
'Blue Prince' (M)
'Blue Wave' (M)
'Domotoi' (M)
'Genérale Vicomtesse de Vibraye' (M)
'Grayswood' (S)
'Hamburg' (M)
'Harlequin' (M)
'Heinrich Seidel' (M)
'Lanarth White' (M)
'Libelle' (M)

'Lilacina' (M)
'Mariesii' (M)
'Masja' (M)
'Mathilda Gutges' (M)
'Merritt's Supreme' (M)
'Mme Emile Mouillère' (M)
'Nikko Blue' (M)
'Otaksa' (M)
'Paris' (M)
'Président Doumer' (M)
'Preziosa' (S)
'Seafoam' (M)
'Tokyo Delight' (M)

Appendix II: Remontant hydrangeas— ideal for cold regions

'Ami Pasquier'
'All Summer Beauty'
'Bodansee'
'Dooley'
'Endless Summer'
'Gartenbaudirektor Kühnert'

'Générale Vicomtesse de Vibraye'
'Glyn Church'
'Libelle'
'Luvumama'
'Marechal Foch'
'Nikko Blue'

Appendix III: Organizations and Suppliers

Organizations

American Hydrangea Society
PO Box 11645
Atlanta, GA
30355-1645, USA
www.americanhydrangeasociety.org

Arboretum Kalmthout
B 2180 Kalmthout, Belgium
Phone: +32 3 666 67 41
Fax: +32 3 666 33 96
www.arboretumkalmthout.be
*Hydrangeas collected and bred
by Jelena de Belder*

Belgium Hydrangea Society
c/- Luc Balemans
Veldekensstraat 40, 9070
Destelbergen, Belgium
Phone/Fax: +32 9 355 71 83
www.hydrangeum.be

British National Collection of Hydrangeas
Lakeland Horticultural Society
Holehird, Patterdale Road
Windermere
Cumbria
England, LA23 1NP
Phone: +44 1539 446 008
www.holehirdgardens.org.uk

Savill Gardens
Windsor Great Park, Windsor
Berkshire
England, SL4 1PJ
Phone: +44 1753 860 222
www.theroyallandscape.co.uk

Shamrock Collection
Route de l'Eglise
76119 Varengeville-sur-Mer
France
Phone: +33 2 3585 14 64
Fax: +33 2 3585 30 20
www.hortensias-hydrangea.com

National Collection of Hydrangeas Australia
George Tindale Memorial Gardens
33 Sherbrooke Road
Sherbrooke VIC
Australia 3789
Phone: +61 3 8627 4699
Fax: +61 3 9629 5563
www.parkweb.vic.gov.au

National Collection of Hydrangeas
New Zealand
Woodleigh Gardens
1403 South Road
Oakura
New Plymouth
New Zealand
Phone: +64 6 752 7597
www.woodleigh.co.nz

Suppliers

United States

Forestfarm
990 Tetherow Road
Williams, OR 97544-9599
Phone: (541) 846 7269
Fax: (541) 846 6963
www.forestfarm.com

Hawksridge Farms
PO Box 3349
South Hickory, NC 28603
Phone: (800) 874 4216
www.hawksridgefarms.com

Hydrangea Plus
Box 389
Aurora, OR 97002
Phone: (503) 651 2887
Toll-free: 866 433 7896
www.hydrangeasplus.com

Joy Creek Nursery
20300 NW Watson Road
Scappoose, OR 97056
Phone: (503) 543 7474
Fax: (503) 543 6933
www.joycreek.com

Nantucket Hydrangeas
Box 2579
86 Madaket Road
Nantucket, MA 02584
Phone: (508) 228 2649
www.nantuckethydrangea.com

Nurseries Caroliniana
143 Mims Grove Church Road
N. Augusta, SC 29841
Phone: (803) 279 2707
www.nurcar.com

Spring Meadow Nursery, Inc.
12601 120th Avenue
Grand Haven, MI 49417-9621
Phone: (800) 633 8859
Fax: (800) 224 1628
www.springmeadownursery.com

Wilkerson Mill Gardens
9595 Wilkerson Mill Rdoad
Palmetto, GA 30268
Phone: (770) 463 2400
Fax: (770) 463 9717
www.hydrangea.com

Canada

Pride of Place Plants
674 Cromarty Avenue
Sidney, BC   V8L 5G6
Phone: (250) 656 7963
Fax: (250) 655 0306
www.prideofplaceplants.com

United Kingdom

Burncoose Nurseries
Gwennap, Redruth
Cornwall, TR16 6BJ
Phone: +44 1209 860 316
Fax: +44 1209 860 011
www.burncoose.co.uk

Crûg Farm Plants
Griffith's Crossing
Caernarfon
Gwynedd, LL55 1TU
Wales
Phone: +44 1248 670 232
www.crug-farm.co.uk

Hillier Nurseries
The Stables, Ampfield House
Ampfield, Romsey
Hampshire, SO51 9BQ
Phone: +44 1794 368733
Fax: +44 1794 368813
www.hillier.co.uk

Loder Plants,
Market Garden, Cyder Farm
Lower Beeding, Horsham
West Sussex, RH13 6PP
Phone: +44 1403 891 412
Fax: +44 1403 891 336
www.hydrangea-haven.com

Notcutts Nurseries Ltd
Woodbridge
Suffolk, IP12 4AF
Phone: +44 1394 445 445
Fax: +44 1394 445 389
www.notcuttsnurseries.co.uk

Spinner's Garden
School Lane, Boldre
Lymington
Hampshire, SO41 5QE
Phone: +44 1590 673 347

Australia

The Flower Garden
Shakes Road, Nairne
South Australia 5252
Phone: +61 8 8388 6126
Fax: + 61 8 8388 0450
www.flowergarden.com.au

New Zealand

Woodleigh Gardens
1403 South Road
RD4 New Plymouth
www.woodleigh.co.nz

Further resources

Surrey Hydrangea Festival
in British Columbia:
www.fraservalleybc.com/hydrangeafestival

www.hydrangeashydrangeas.com

Pete's Hydrangeas:
www.conweb.com/hydrangea/

Garden Web's hydrangea forum:
http://forums.gardenweb.com/forums/hydra/

Information on Hovaria® hydrangeas:
www.hovaria.com

Photographic Credits

LUC BALEMANS pages 66, 67 right, 90 lower, 119, 121 two right, 122 top right
MAL CONDON pages 5 top, 62, 63, 84 second and fourth, 87
PAT GREENFIELD front cover and pages 3, 5 (second from top), 6–7, 11, 16 right, 34, 38 right, 40 lower, 42, 48 both, 51, 54, 56, 68 right, 72 right, 75, 76, 80, 86, 91 right, 92 lower, 98 lower, 100 lower, 102, 106 top, 108 top right, 136 left
GIL HANLY pages 8, 9 bottom, 21, 22, 23, 24 both, 25, 27, 29, 30, 41, 46, 47, 58, 61, 70, 73, 77
KOOS and WILKO HOFSTEDE pages 71, 96 left, 99 lower right, 113 lower right
RYOJI IRIE pages 1, 5 middle, 38 top left, 40 top, 72 left, 89 top, 91 two left, 108 top left, 112 two left
JUDITH KING pages 4, 19, 31 both, 38 lower left, 89 lower, 92 top, 125, 139 left
CORINNE MALLET page 114
TOM MILLS pages 2, 106 lower
TIM WOOD pages 33, 79 both, 121 top left, 122 two left
GLYN CHURCH back cover and pages 5 lower two, 9 top and middle, 10, 12 both, 13, 14, 15 both, 16 left, 17, 18, 20, 26, 28, 35, 36, 37, 39, 44, 49 both, 52 both, 59, 60, 64, 67 left, 68 left, 69, 78, 80 top, 81, 82, 83 all, 84 first and third, 85, 88 both, 90 top, 93, 94, 95 both, 96 right, 97, 98 top, 99 left and top, 100 top, 101 both, 103 all, 104, 105 both, 107, 108 lower, 109, 110, 111 both, 112 right, 113 left and top two right, 115 both, 116, 117, 118 both, 120 both, 124, 126 all, 128 both, 129 both, 130 both, 131, 132, 133 both, 134 both, 136 right, 137, 138, 139 two right

Bibliography

Adriaenssen, Diane and Robert de Belder. *Generous as Nature Herself*. Brussels: Editions d'Art Laconti, 2006.
Church, Glyn. *Hydrangeas: A gardener's guide*. Toronto: Firefly Books, 1999.
Coates, Alice. *The Quest for Plants: A history of the horticultural explorers*. London: Studio Vista, 1969.
Condon, Mal. *Love Those Paniculatas*. Grayson: The American Hydrangea Society, 2003.
Dirr, Michael. *Hydrangeas for American Gardens*. Portland: Timber Press, 2004.
Haworth-Booth, Michael. *The Hydrangeas* (5th edition). London: Constable, 1984.
Hillier, H.G. *The Hillier Manual of Trees and Shrubs*. Newton Abbott: David & Charles, 1991.
Krussman, Gerd. *A Manual of Cultivated Broad Leaved Trees and Shrubs*. Portland: Timber Press, 1984.
Lawson-Hall, Toni and Brian Rothera. *Hydrangeas: A gardener's guide*. London: Batsford, 1995.
Mallet, Corinne. *Hydrangeas: Species and cultivars* (vols 1 and 2). Varengeville-sur-Mer: Centre d'Art Floral, 1994.
Pizetti, I. and Cocker, H. *Flowers: A guide for your garden*. New York: Abrams, 1975.
Tripp, Kim E. and J. C. Raulston. *The Year in Trees*. Portland: Timber Press, 1995.
van Gelderen, C.J. and D.M. *Encyclopedia of Hydrangeas*. Portland: Timber Press, 2004.
Whittle, Tyler. *The Plant Hunters*. London: Heinemann, 1970.

Index

AUTHOR'S ACKNOWLEDGMENTS

Writing about Feng Shui always gives me enormous pleasure but seeing my manuscript transformed into this stunningly beautiful book just takes my breath away, for which I truly must thank Element Books.

To Sonia Land, my agent, must go the credit for seeing the great promise of a tie-up with Element Books. To Julia McCutchen a huge hug for her vision; to Caro Ness a warm embrace for her patience and sensitivity and to the team at the Bridgewater Book Company grateful acknowledgement of their creativity and meticulous attention to detail.

I must also acknowledge all the Feng Shui experts whose input progressively enhanced my knowledge of this great science as they successively passed through my life – but most of all, I owe a huge debt of gratitude to Master Yap Cheng Hai, my friend and Si Fu for his wonderful generosity in sharing Feng Shui kung fu (wisdom), and secret computations with me, formulas that successfully provided the key to unlocking Feng Shui's many complexities . . . I am so enormously grateful to him. And finally, to all my readers and friends in Malaysia and in Singapore. It was their support and encouragement that provided the impetus for me to carry on writing.

LILLIAN TOO

Grateful acknowledgment must go to Thomas Wang for the material on Feng Shui and western science on pages 30–33 which is an abridged version of his essay.

Lillian Too may be contacted on: The World Wide Web URL http://www.asiaconnect.com.my/lillian-too
or http://www.wwwmktg.com/fengshui/ *or E-mail* ltoo@asiaconnect.com.my *or* ltoo@jaring.com.my

PUBLISHER'S ACKNOWLEDGMENTS

The publishers wish to thank the following for the use of pictures:
Ancient Art & Architecture Collection: pp.13R, 31B, 75TL
Berita Publishing Sdn. Bhd. (Her World Home Scene magazine, vol 1, 1994): pp.60L, 61, 67L, 67R
Bridgeman Art Library: pp.62, 86 (Victoria & Albert Museum)
Christie's Images: pp.8/9
e.t.archive: pp.65T, 162B, 209; 19B, 25 (National Palace Museum, Taiwan); 23 (Science Museum, London); 50 (William Rockhill Nelson Gallery, Kansas); 167L (Brera Milan); 212 (Victoria & Albert Museum); 213 (British Museum)
The Garden Picture Library: pp.46 (Brian Carter); 60TR (Juliette Wade); 60BR (Henk Dickman)
Habitat: pp.170BL, 170BCL, 170BCR, 170BR, 171L, 171TR, 171BR
Hulton Deutsch Collection Ltd: pp.27T, 207B; 37 (Ross Kinnaird)
The Image Bank: pp.136BL; 2/3 (Tadao Kimura); 10 (estudio Francisco Rajo); 12T, 17BR (Jeff Spielman); 12B, 17BCL, 146R, 146L,178T (Romilly Lockyer); 16BL (Alan Becker); 16BR (M Pasdzior); 17BL (Michael Salas); 17BCR (D Berwin); 28, 33, 59R (P & G Bowater); 31T (Steve Satushek); 34 (Antonio M Rosario); 36B (Real Life); 38 (Marc Grimberg); 41T (Marvin E Newman); 43B (Steve Allen); 48/49 (Zhen Ge Peng); 53R, 180 (Grant V Faint); 54L (Rob Atkins); 58 (Peter Frey); 59L (B Martin); 64L, 166BL (Harald Sund); 69T (Zao Grimberg); 87, 136TL (Kaz Mori); 96B (Gary Ross); 98T, 99L (Yellow Dog Prods); 106/107 (Pete Turner); 109B, 136BC (Hans Wolf); 109T (Derek Redfearn); 110 (Antony Edwards); 112 (Terje Rakke); 113T (Nick Pavloff); 114L (Gary Cralle); 114R (F Roiter); 116B (Cesar Lucas); 118L (Jun Ling); 136TR (Ancrea Pistolesi); 136BR, 148BL (Steve Dunwell); 138 (Dag Sundberg); 139R (F Rojo Alvarez); 144L (A Choisnet); 144R (Tom Knibbs); 145BR (H Willig); 146CL (Ivor Wood); 146CR (Herb Hartmann); 147L (Stephen Marks); 147CL (Robert Morris); 147CR, 184BL, 207T (Infocus International); 147R (Eddie Hironaka); 153TL (Patti McConville); 157R (Chuck Lawliss); 172/173 (David Brownell); 174 (Patrick Doherty); 178B (Hank de Lespinasse); 179 (Jeff Hunter); 179R (John Banagan); 193B (Miguel Martin); 206 (James Meyer)
Images Colour Library: p.202
The Kobal Collection: pp.203B, 203T
The Stock House Ltd: pp.18; 26 (James Montgomery); 29T (Steve Vidler); 117T (Dallas & John Heaton); 175 (Timothy Liu)
Syndication International: pp.36R
Lillian Too: pp.7, 47
Zefa Picture Library: pp.11R, 19T, 43T, 65R, 69B, 89TR, 105B, 108, 111T, 115R, 117B, 118/119, 120, 126, 127T, 139L, 145T, 168L, 211; 24, 142 (J Becker); 30 (Davies); 115L (Naegele); 127B (Barone); 152L (Grinsven); 153BL (F Thomas); 160 (Schi Aback); 210L (A Edgeworth)

Special thanks go to:
Bonsai-Ko, Brighton, East Sussex
Bright Ideas, Lewes, East Sussex
Dixons Ltd, Lewes, East Sussex
Habitat Designs Ltd
Vokins, Brighton, East Sussex
for help with properties.

S

schools/theories, 62, 104–105
  Compass School, 22–23, 24, 63–64, 84, 87
  Flying Star Feng Shui, 105
  Form School, 21, 57, 63, 87
  Four Pillars method, 25
  Pa-Kua Lo-Shu theory, 25, 98–103
  Water Dragon theory, 25, 105, 121, 157, 187
science, 30–33, 85, 213
seasons, 52, 71, 105
shade, 21, 60–61, 114
Shar Chi, 12, 29, 32, 136, 213
  countering, 41, 42
  doorways, 16
  towns/cities, 59
Sheng Chi, 12, 65, 68–69, 110, 113, 213
signboards, 189
Singapore, 11, 14, 15, 35, 165
sleeping, 13
  direction, 38, 67, 134, 194, 207
  illness, 210, 211
  location, 70, 102, 141, 150, 207
space dimension, 53, 64–65, 84
staircases, 28, 144–145, 181
stock markets, 26, 41, 123
stove, 211
  location, 92, 97
  position, 96, 99, 102, 154
study, 80, 134, 141, 144
Sun Yat Sen, 28
sunlight, 21, 52, 60–61, 114
swimming pools, 156–157
symbols, 30, 65, 104
  animals, 13, 20–21, 44, 84, 118–119, 161
  Compass School, 22–23, 63
  good fortune, 13, 66–67, 161–162
  interpretation, 25, 46, 57
  trigrams, 76–77

T

tables, 45, 154, 170, 185
Taiwan, 11, 14, 24, 29, 35, 175
Tao, 51, 53, 85
texts, 18–20, 47, 105, 134, 157
tiger
  green dragon/white tiger formation, 21, 56, 63, 64, 109, 178
  landscape, 21, 56, 57, 69, 109–111
  symbolism, 19, 30, 33, 84
  Yin, 52
time dimension, 53, 64, 87, 105
toilet, 103, 152–153, 154, 180
  career success, 194
  location, 92, 94, 180
  marriage/family corners, 39, 80, 148, 203, 205, 209
Tong Shu, 85
topography, 19, 20, 24, 33, 56
tortoise, 13, 20, 33, 69
trees, 55, 176
  deflecting poison arrows, 43
  as poison arrows, 12, 136, 137
  as protection, 112, 113, 115, 117
trigrams
  I Ching 63, 65, 72, 73, 74–77
  Pa-Kua 22, 84, 141
turtle
  Lo Shu Magic Square, 84
  symbolism, 13, 20, 33, 56, 69, 109–111

V

vegetation, 21, 113, 124

W

walls, 61, 117, 159
water, 11
  business premises, 184, 186–187, 188
  Chi impact, 68
  in garden, 60, 156
  in landscape, 54, 69, 87, 110–112, 117, 120–121
  pools/ponds, 156–157
  symbolism, 13, 15, 70–71, 77
  towns/cities, 58
  Yin, 52
Water Dragon formula, 25, 105, 121, 157, 187
wealth, 11, 32, 66, 80
  business, life 102, 186–187
  god of, 166
  Pa Kua, 78, 81, 83
  symbols, 13, 120
weather, 33, 113, 114–115
Western countries, 16–17
White House, Washington D.C., 13
wind, 11, 33, 109, 129
  Chi impact, 68
  protection, 56, 69, 113, 115
wind chimes, 46, 71, 135
  beams, 45, 143
  business premises, 188, 189
  career success, 195
  corners, 45, 143
  enhancers, 80, 82
windows, 128, 130, 134–135
Winter Palace, Russia, 145
wisdom, 13
wood, symbolism, 70–71, 76–77
woodworking business, 189

Y

Yang Dwelling Classic, 134, 154
yard, 60, 129, 156, 159
Yin and Yang, 21, 50–61, 72–73, 113